Not About Being Good is a skilful book about how to be ethical, full of personal material that is easy to identify with as well as wise stories that give one valuable food for thought. The style is lively and easy to read. The author's own struggles with the issues are disarmingly revealed as the book takes the reader on a progressive journey from scepticism to confidence and from confusion to more robust practice.

David Brazier, president of the International Zen Therapy Institute, head of the Amida Order, author of *Not Everything is Impermanent*

In *Not About Being Good*, Subhadramati brings Buddhist ethics to life, for real people living in the real world. Drawing on her extensive experience of practising and teaching, she brings her unique gifts to the subject. Subhadramati has a wonderful perspective on life: she is in touch with a river running beneath the surface of things, aware of the wonder of being alive. Yet the pragmatist dwells comfortably alongside the poet, and this makes her a realistic and sympathetic guide to ethics in the twenty-first century. Here you will find exercises to help you build confidence in how Buddhist ethics can provide a fool-proof map for life, and you will discover great riches along the way.

Vidyamala Burch, co-founder and director of Breathworks, author of *Living Well with Pain and Illness* and *Mindfulness for Health*

This book does an excellent job in placing ethics and meditation at the heart of Buddhist practice, and shows how they work together in transforming ordinary human beings into Buddhas.

Professor Damien Keown, co-founder of *The Journal of Buddhist Ethics*, author of *The Nature of Buddhist Ethics*

Not About Being Good is a practical, unpreachy introduction to why ethics matters and how to make the best of life. Writing with passion, humour and delicacy, gloriously free from moralism, Subhadramati's aim is to help us live a richer and fuller life.

Maitreyabandhu, author of *Life with Full Attention* and *The Journey and the Guide*

This accessible book enables the reader to understand something of Buddhist ethics through reflection and meditation; it is 'a practical guide', rejecting notions of good and bad in favour of developing awareness of the intentions that underpin actions and words.

Joyce Miller, *REtoday*

T0273295

Not About Being Good

a practical guide to buddhist ethics

Subhadramati

Published by
Windhorse Publications
38 Newmarket Road
Cambridge
CB5 8DT
UK

info@windhorsepublications.com
www.windhorsepublications.com

Cover design by Dhammarati

Permission has been granted for the use of all images, as noted in the List of Figures.

Typeset and designed by Ben Cracknell Studios

British Library Cataloguing in Publication Data:
A catalogue record for this book is available from the British Library.

ISBN: 978 1 909314 01 6

For my parents who gave me life and for Dhammarati who introduced me to the Buddha.

....

About the author

Subhadramati has been a Buddhist for over twenty-five years and joined the Triratna Buddhist Order in 1995. She worked in Buddhist team-based right-livelihood businesses (a restaurant and a gift-shop) in London and Dublin for seventeen years before starting to work full-time at the London Buddhist Centre. At the LBC she particularly works with women wanting to explore and deepen Buddhist practice, as well as teaching meditation and Buddhism more generally. She lives with eleven other Buddhist women in a residential Buddhist community.

Acknowledgements

The first sparks of inspiration for this book came when I gave a series of talks on Buddhist ethics on a three-month women's ordination retreat in the Spanish mountains in 2007. The women on that retreat encouraged me to write up those talks into a book, but it was only when I was approached by Priyananda of Windhorse Publications in the summer of 2011 that I finally gathered my energies sufficiently to do so.

Neither those talks nor this book, however, would have been possible without my teacher Urgyen Sangharakshita, whose guidance I am continually and ever more deeply grateful for. I hope I have been faithful to his teaching. I am also grateful to Subhuti, one of the most senior members of the Triratna Buddhist Order; his recent writings have influenced this book substantially.

This book owes a great deal to the London Buddhist Centre. Being part of the vibrant teaching team there helps me to clarify and deepen my understanding, as does the atmosphere of interest and enquiry at our classes. My gratitude goes to all involved.

I take this opportunity to thank my editors Jnanasiddhi and Priyananda for all their help and encouragement, Dhatvisvari for her beautiful polishing of the text, and also all the team at Windhorse Publications. Thanks too to Dhammarati for his cover design, which shows us that when conventional morality is looked at afresh, something unexpected is revealed, to Jinamitra for the generous use of his studio facilities in recording the led meditations and reflections, and to Subhadra for his generous editing of the recordings. I want to thank Vajrasakhi for reading the draft and making astute comments. And my sister Maureen Healy for being my 'jargon-buster'. I also thank the other eleven women in my community for giving me practical support and keeping me on track. And finally thanks to my old friend Maitreyabandhu for helping me to know what I meant.

Publisher's acknowledgement

Windhorse Publications wishes to gratefully acknowledge a grant from the Triratna European Chairs' Assembly Fund towards the production of this book.

Audio downloads

This book has been produced with accompanying guided meditations and reflections by the author, available as free downloads. They are marked with a 🔔, and can be streamed directly from the Web or downloaded in MP3 format. Please go to bit.ly/notaboutbeinggood or windhorsepublications.com/not-about-being-good-audio.

Terms of use

The publisher grants to individuals who purchased *Not About Being Good* non-assignable permission to stream and download the audio files on the Web page, as designated. This licence is limited to you, the individual user, for personal use only. This licence does not grant the right to reproduce these materials for resale, redistribution, broadcast, or any other purposes (including but not limited to books, pamphlets, articles, video or audiotapes, blogs, file-sharing sites, Internet or intranet sites, and handouts or slides for lectures, workshops, webinars, or therapy groups, whether or not a fee is charged) in audio form or in transcription. Permission to reproduce these materials for these and any other purposes must be obtained in writing from Windhorse Publications.

Contents

List of figures

Introduction

As a child I used to go to chapel a lot. As well as morning mass on Sundays, I'd go to rosary and benediction on Sunday evenings, mass every morning before school, and confession on Saturdays. But I'd often go on my own too, when the chapel was empty and quiet, not so much to pray as to reflect, with all the intensity particular to eleven-year-old Catholic girls. One morning, while I was trying to visualize the glories of heaven, I was overwhelmed by the thought that God was just an invention constructed by humans to explain things they didn't yet understand. Feeling the very structure of everything I'd built my inner life around crumbling away, I tried as hard as I could to push this intrusive thought away. But I was powerless in the face of it. This was a pivotal moment. Remembering it now, I can still see exactly which pew I was kneeling in – next to the Station of the Cross where Veronica wipes the face of Jesus – and I can vividly recall my dismay.

The big questions

After that I still went to chapel but the heart had gone out of my devotions. As I entered my teens I turned away from religion altogether, and towards science. I reckoned that if God had just been an explanation for everything in the universe that wasn't understood, then surely science, particularly the study of physics, would be a better bet in trying to find wisdom in relation to life's mysteries. I put my hopes on science to provide me with the answers to questions that all began with the word 'Why?' But after four years at university, although I gained an honours degree in natural philosophy (as the study of pure physics was called in Scottish universities), and could get my head around mathematical formulas that could fill half this page, I was just another mixed-up twenty-one-year-old. I put my failure to find 'answers' down to just not being clever enough. But when, a year or so later, I met my first Buddhist guides, I revised the very questions I was seeking answers for. Rather than focusing on why the universe is as it is, the crucial issue became how I should live my life within it.

The immediate appeal to me of this new 'how-to'-based approach was that (in theory at least) no matter how confused my mind, or how turbulent my emotions, there was always something I could do; it was a practical, hands-on approach. But, even more than that, as I started to follow the Buddhist teachings that were offered, I began to see that real wisdom is not something you can think about in abstract or even metaphysical terms. I began to see that it's not something you can 'have' – no matter how fervently you think or how clever you are. I began to see that wisdom encompasses all your actually lived attitudes, all your behaviour.

This then is a book about actually lived attitudes and behaviour. It is a book about Buddhist ethics. My own Buddhist teacher, Sangharakshita, founder of the Triratna Buddhist Community and Order, has written and taught about Buddhist ethics over many years, and one of my main aims in writing this book is to bring together some of those teachings from different sources – books, lectures, and unpublished study seminars[1] – that have helped and inspired me, in the hope that they will inspire you too. As well as exploring the spirit of the Buddhist approach to ethics, this book is a practical guide to ethics.

There's a Buddhist story about a monk who lives in the mountains. Every so often he comes down to the marketplace. One day a rather arrogant stallholder disparagingly asks, 'What on earth do you do up there in the mountains all day?' The monk, unphased, smiles and says, 'In the mountains it is very beautiful, there are wild forests to roam in and clear lakes to swim in. But I can't bring those forests and lakes down to you; you'll have to come up the mountain and see for yourself.' The monk of course is talking about the inner joy he dwells in by living the renunciate's life. It's impossible to convey it in words; it has to be experienced first-hand. It's the same with this book. I can perhaps give you a glimpse of my own inspiration and enthusiasm for Buddhist practice, particularly the practice of Buddhist ethics. But to really know where Buddhist ethics spring from and where they are pointing to, you'll have to try them out for yourself. Throughout the book I've made suggestions for reflections and suggestions for practical exercises that you can do in your everyday life. It's these reflections and exercises that will be the real teachers. It's these, if you're up for giving them a go, that will allow you to 'see for yourself'.

A truly human life

The trouble with writing a book about Buddhist ethics, compared with, say, a book on Buddhist meditation or Buddhist wisdom, is that people often already have strong associations with the concept of ethics – and these are often negative.

One of the negative ways we can think about ethics is perhaps evoked by the story the main character, David Lurie, tells in J.M. Coetzee's novel *Disgrace*. It's the story of a dog, a male golden retriever, that would get excited and unmanageable whenever there was a bitch in the vicinity. Every single time this happened the owners would beat it. This went on until the poor dog no longer knew what to do. Eventually, even at the smell of a bitch, it would chase round the garden with its tail between its legs, whining, trying to hide. It didn't need to be beaten anymore: it was ready to punish itself. It had become afraid of – and started to hate – its own nature. Lurie's daughter asks if it wouldn't have been better to just castrate the dog, which makes Lurie despair even more. He's sure the dog would have preferred to be shot rather than being 'fixed' and spending the rest of its life padding about the living room.[2]

If you think of ethics in these terms, as having to keep your own nature under control, or as something imposed upon you and kept in place by a system of reward and punishment (more punishment than reward for the poor dog it seems), or, even worse, as having to be 'fixed' in order to conform to someone else's idea of 'good behaviour', then it won't be surprising if you have negative associations.

In Buddhism, being ethical means learning to act more and more in accordance with your values. Buddhist ethics are very far from the kind of system that makes us suspicious of our own natures, and calls on us to distort our own natures. Buddhist ethics don't see human nature as something that has to be beaten into submission, tamed, or domesticated. Buddhism is not trying 'steadfastly to cure life of itself'.[3] Buddhism is about fulfilling our human nature, not diminishing or even crippling it, and Buddhist ethics are both part of the way to that fulfilment and the expression of that fulfilment. The word 'ethics' comes from the Greek 'ethos', which in modern English can be translated as 'the character of an individual as represented by his or her values and beliefs'.[4]

It might seem strange to be told that you have to learn to act in accordance with your values. But sometimes it is difficult to know what your own values are. They can get mixed up with the values of some authority or perceived authority; they can get mixed up with your conventional assumptions about what morality is; or they can be mixed up with religious rites and rituals. It's easy to be unconsciously influenced by ideas about what is normal in a particular group or culture. For example, it was only when my Jewish friend's Catholic son-in-law refused to have his new baby son ritually circumcised that she stopped to think about something she'd simply taken for granted until then. She told me, 'It was just what you did. It was what made you part of the community.' At first she was as horrified by the thought of it not taking place as her son-in-law was at the thought of it happening. But then she reflected that maybe there was something in what he was saying too. She even remembered her own feelings of distress at the time of her son's circumcision. The whole incident made her look again at something she had taken on unquestioningly as a good thing in and of itself and see it in a different way, from more points of view.

In these kinds of situations society itself then becomes, without your being aware of it, the 'authority' persuading you to conform by rewarding you when you do conform, and by punishing you when you don't. The trouble is, because each brand of conventional moral system becomes the norm within the culture, it is easy to take it on unthinkingly. By definition, the rules and everyday conventions of morality differ from place to place and time to time. So you can suddenly spot them for what they are when you encounter people from cultures, class backgrounds, or religious backgrounds different from your own. For example in India it would be considered indecent for a husband and wife to hold hands in public but perfectly acceptable for male friends to do so, whereas in the UK the opposite is true – a man and a woman can hold hands and even kiss in public, but two men holding hands is considered indecent.

Of course conventional morality may sometimes align with natural morality. The key thing is that, if you want to discover what truly human values are, you'll have to continually be on the lookout for values that you've adopted unthinkingly. These may be to do with what, when, and how you eat; who you sleep with; what you spend your money on; how you bring up your children or care for your elderly parents. In other words, you'll have to continually be on the lookout for moments when you are swayed or influenced by mere convention. If you cultivate this kind of sensibility you'll find that you clear the way for the growth of what Sangharakshita has called 'natural morality'.

Natural morality springs out of the awareness that other people are essentially no different from ourselves. They, like us, have hopes, fears, people they care about, and a desire to be fulfilled in life. Crucially, Buddhism recognizes that the potential for this awareness is part of the structure of human consciousness. It's what we call conscience and it comes with being human. Because Buddhism recognizes that this potential for imaginative identification with others is innate, the teachings of Buddhism are not there to generate our moral sense but to lead it out, to educate it.[5]

The teachings are necessary because, although they're innate, our naturally ethical impulses, that is those based on imaginative identification with others, are competing with our other impulses. They become hidden by, or mixed up, with 'conventional ethics'. They get buried when we allow the opposite tendencies of this imaginative identification to develop by making certain choices or finding (or putting) ourselves in certain conditions. They get reduced or 'blunted' when we don't make conscious efforts to put them into practice.[6] In this book, as well as introducing teachings, I'll be suggesting ways to approach those teachings. And I'll be reminding you throughout that, in Buddhism, being ethical means being truly human.

Ethics, meditation, wisdom

In practice, in the West at least, most people come to Buddhist centres primarily to learn to meditate. Many, at least at first, have no more than a passing interest in Buddhism. Others are quite definitely wary about anything that smacks of 'organized religion'; this was certainly true of me at first.

Now, however, I teach meditation on Wednesday evenings at our drop-in class at the London Buddhist Centre. We run classes all week, all year; whether it's the school holidays or Christmas time. We ran them during the week of the UK riots in 2011 when the local shops barricaded their windows and police sirens wailed outside the shrine-room. And we ran them during the weeks of the London Olympics in 2012, when strangers got into conversations with each other in the parks. Before I say anything about meditation, I usually ask the people in the class what's motivated them to come along. And invariably, whatever time of year it is, whatever's going on outside, whatever news is in the papers, I get a similar set of responses to my question. Very occasionally someone says they have come to explore the spiritual dimension of life. Now and then there may be someone who has an inkling that meditation might help stop her getting so annoyed with her boss all the time. Nearly always someone will hesitantly admit that they've heard meditation can help with anxiety or depression, and several others will nod. But most of the people, most of the time, say they want to reduce stress and to feel calmer. They want to learn how to quieten their minds, especially amidst the frenetic pace of living in a big city.

All these motives are good ones, and I always assure people that, although the meditations we teach are firmly rooted in the Buddhist tradition, no one has to be a Buddhist or even interested in Buddhism to practise them and benefit from them. At the same time I know that if anyone seriously takes up meditation, sooner or later, quite naturally, practising it will lead them to consider and even reconsider their actions in accordance with their values. Furthermore, for some, again quite naturally, meditation will lead them to ponder on the existential situation in which we all find ourselves. In other words, quite naturally, the practice of meditation will lead into the more overarching arena of what Buddhism calls the 'threefold path' of ethics, meditation, and wisdom.

Here are a couple of examples to illustrate the natural connection between meditation and ethics. The first is from my own life. After I'd just learnt to meditate and been practising meditation regularly for a few months, I started suddenly and inexplicably to feel nauseous within moments of sitting down on my cushions and closing my eyes. It got so bad that I'd have to get up immediately and abandon the meditation. Eventually I told the meditation-class leader, convinced he'd give me some instructions about the technique that I could put into practice right away to fix this problem. But he didn't say anything about the way I was meditating at all. Instead he looked at me kindly and asked what sort of things were going on in the rest of my life (I was twenty-three years old at the time). I was astonished by this question; it wasn't what I'd expected at all. But, perhaps because he was looking at me so kindly, I blurted out that I wasn't being honest in my personal life. 'But', I added emphatically, 'I can't see how that's got anything to do with my meditation.' He just carried on gazing kindly and the truth gradually dawned. The unease and nausea I was experiencing had everything to do with how I was living my life. I went away and began to sort out the mess I'd got into. This was the beginning of me realizing that what I get up to in the rest of my life has everything to do with my meditation and that meditation has everything to do with what I get up to in the rest of my life; they can't be treated as separate activities.

The spotlight of awareness that meditation can shine upon our lives is not always entirely welcome. A friend of mine, Canute, had joined a gang at the age of thirteen and by the time he was fifteen he'd been in juvenile detention facilities. By his twenties he was living a life of hard drinking and fighting, working as a doorman in London's nightclubs, which he described as 'just waiting for something to happen so you can just slam out'. Then a chance meeting with an old friend rekindled his interest in philosophy. As a result of this he came to the Buddhist Centre and learnt to meditate. He took to meditation straight away because 'it was like smoking a spliff without smoking a spliff'. Wednesdays, when he came to the Centre, became his 'holy day'. He didn't drink or smoke because he wanted to have a clear mind so he could sit and meditate. But before long he realized he was going to have to make more radical changes. He said, 'I couldn't continue to meditate and change my inner state without having to change what was going on outside.' He realized that drinking whisky and looking for fights had to stop altogether. These days he shakes his head (although he can't disguise his grin) when he says, 'Meditation is dangerous because you're forced to look at yourself, forced to change; in a certain respect, meditation has ruined my life.'

I hope these examples show that practising meditation, because it's about becoming more aware, will start to clarify your natural ethical sense. It will 'sharpen' your sense of conscience. It will unbury it and bring it to life. If you take up meditation with any degree of seriousness, you will realize that meditating regularly becomes more and more incompatible with acting in ways that harm others or yourself. As Canute says, 'It would have been easy to go back to the drinking and fighting – all I'd have had to do was give up meditating.'

I'll be exploring the natural connection of ethics and meditation with wisdom, the third step in the threefold path, in more detail in Chapters 7 and 8. For now, the main point to make clear is that, although the threefold path is progressive, starting with ethics, and certainly to sustain any serious development of a further stage you will need a strong foundation in the earlier stage, it's not as if ethics and meditation are building bricks to be plonked on top of each other. It is more organic than that. If you're practising meditation, your ethical sensibility will become more attuned. As a result of that, your actual practice of ethics will become stronger. This in turn will act as a further support for your meditation, because your meditation will be less disturbed by conflicting emotions. So by practising both meditation and ethics (and if you haven't already learnt to meditate, I'd suggest exploring the possibility of learning), you'll start to create a positive feedback loop where each will support the deepening of the other.

Practising the art

In terms of ethics, not only will your values become clearer to you as you become more aware, they will deepen as your ethical sensibility becomes more attuned, as you become more ethically sensitive. So

Not About Being Good

far I've talked about this happening in an organic way. But it's also something you can develop and cultivate the way you might develop and cultivate any art or skill.

In fact, rather than talking about actions being 'good' or 'bad', Buddhism talks about them being skilful – the Buddhist words are kusala ('skilful') and akusala ('unskilful'). What determines whether an action is skilful or unskilful is not just the action itself, but the intention underlying the act. Actions that are expressions of generosity towards others, love, goodwill towards them, or wisdom are kusala. And those that are expressions of selfishness towards others, ill-will or hatred towards them, or delusion are akusala. So your mental states are the governing factor, rather than some predefined rule of what is 'good' and what is 'bad'. This means that Buddhism does not provide – or try to enforce – an overarching moral code for everyone collectively to abide by. Instead Buddhism teaches that each of us must take individual and personal responsibility for our actions. So, for example, when the Dalai Lama was asked how he felt about the self-immolation of Tibetans as acts of protest, first of all he was careful to say that the fact that they would harm themselves instead of harming others demonstrated a commitment to non-violence. However, he went on to say that if such an action was driven by anger and hatred it would be basically negative, whereas it would not be negative if the motivation was 'mainly a more compassionate one of sincere faith in Buddha-Dharma'.[7]

This emphasis on individual and personal responsibility is quite different from the message we often hear in 'religious' arguments, which is that without a framework made up of absolute standards there can be no genuine moral conduct (even though it isn't hard to observe that not all 'religious' people are 'good' and not all 'good' people are 'religious'). It can feel liberating – I know it did for me – to discover that practising Buddhist ethics isn't about avoiding certain proscribed activities, but about developing skilful intentions. However, there's a challenge involved here too because the only way to learn a skill is by actually practising it – no one else can do that for you.

Every time I go into a bookshop I'm struck by how the cookbook section seems to be ever-expanding. There are hundreds of cookbooks, each glossier than the last. But at the same time supermarket shelves seem to be more and more stocked with 'ready meals', suggesting that, although people buy more and more cookbooks, they actually cook less and less. Just owning lots of cookbooks won't make you a cook. Even if you read them you'll only learn in a limited way. I know this because I'm one of the people who probably spend more time flicking through recipes than actually making them. What I have noticed, however, is that the cookbooks themselves can be of two types. Some focus on precise lists of ingredients, timings, and oven temperatures. In others though, the author tries to communicate the art and the heart of cooking, tries to inspire you to get a feel for it, to catch the spirit of it so that you'll be able to respond and adapt to changes in circumstances – whether that's missing ingredients, unexpected guests, your own moods, or the weather outside. He's trying to give you confidence so you won't automatically lose heart when something is more difficult than you thought it would be. And he's hoping you'll find ways of being creative that are brand new – that if you ever met him, you could teach him! In these books the instructions will be less precise – and sometimes even seemingly contradictory.

Edward Brown, of the Tassajara[8] cookbooks, says that he sees his task as teaching people not just to follow recipes, but to awaken their own capacity to respond to circumstances, to go beyond getting it right, and to make food alive with their aliveness. You can see he's trying to empower people, not just get people to do what he tells them. He says:

> … if you have the heart for it, while you work on cooking, cooking will work on you, and refine you, so that you come out of the fire even more large-hearted.[9]

Like a cookbook, this book is intended to be a practical book. I hope it will inspire you to practise ethics more and more creatively. And like the Tassajara cookbooks, it doesn't emphasize 'recipes'. You won't find any rules about whether you should stop flying on aeroplanes, start drinking soya milk, stop letting your kids play the Xbox, start giving money to that homeless woman you see near the subway entrance every day, donate your vital organs. Instead, I hope that it will help you to awaken more fully your own capacity to respond to

Not About Being Good

circumstances and situations with creativity and intelligence. This book offers a set of principles and practices, tried and tested over 2,500 years, so that, as you work on your ethics, your practice of ethics will work on you, and you will come out of the fire larger-hearted and wiser.

A to-do list for life

Years ago when I worked in a Buddhist gift-shop in Dublin I enjoyed spending my lunch hour in a particular basement second-hand bookshop. I loved the fact that, while up at street level the pavements would be thronging with shoppers, down in the basement it would be peaceful and almost church-like. I particularly remember leafing through a volume of poetry and finding a handwritten page torn from a notepad. It was a to-do list that read:

> Buy an alarm clock.
> Collect screwdrivers.
> Don't forget Lucy's birthday.
> Try to be less selfish today.

The words on that list have stayed with me. I'll never know the author of them, so I always think of him as 'Everyman' listing his tasks for the day. I'm sure the list helped in remembering the clock, the screwdrivers, and the birthday. But did the list-writer manage to be less selfish that day? I don't doubt the sincerity of the wish – in fact it's because of the sincerity of the wish that I've remembered that list for all this time. But I know from my own experience how difficult it is to be unselfish for even a single day. I set out to be unselfish, I really want to be unselfish – I can see that's best – but when it comes to it the moment overwhelms me and I forget. We can be so caught up in the everyday with its tasks and e-mails that we just forget that the thing we really meant to do was to be generous, kind, thoughtful. We forget the thing we really meant to do was to be less selfish. It can be difficult to even imagine what an unselfish state of mind might be like. When whoever it was wrote that note, he must have really meant it, wished for it, seen that that was best – but it almost certainly got forgotten as the note itself was forgotten.

Buddhism would say you're right to wish to be less selfish, and you're right that that's the most important thing, but you need a guide, a practice, a supportive context, and a path to successfully achieve that. Buddhism says it is possible to reach a truly unselfish state of mind and to act from that basis – not just for one day but consistently. Buddhism describes genuine unselfishness as a dynamic and positive state – a state of unlimited creativity. Practising Buddhist ethics is a path towards this kind of unselfish spontaneous responsiveness. It's a step-by-step practical path – not really so different from remembering to buy an alarm clock or making sure you have the right type of screwdriver.

I've written this book to help the person who left that note to live from that wish to be less selfish. I've written it for anyone who wants – in addition to getting up for work in time, fixing that shelf with that screwdriver, remembering to send that birthday card – to be in touch with a spirit of unselfishness, of love, of pure response.

How to use this book

The chapters in this book are arranged to take you through the steps of this practical path. You could say ethics has three levels. First of all you realize that it's in your own interests to act unselfishly. You realize that practising ethics will lead to greater happiness and satisfaction for yourself, so you take on the practice in that spirit. There may be a struggle but, as you see the benefits, you become more and more convinced the struggle is worth it. I cover this level in Chapter 1. The second level of ethics springs out of your natural empathy for the world around you and your wish not to cause harm. I explore this in Chapter 2. In the third and highest level of ethics you no longer experience selfish motivations at all. To move from the second to the third level involves a complete reorientation of your being. It involves receptivity to those wiser than yourself. It requires commitment. And it involves learning to let go of your instinctive self-referential mode of seeing things so that you can see things just as they are without 'you' in the centre of everything. How to bring about this reorientation takes more understanding, so I have dedicated the remaining chapters to that.

Each chapter in this book contains a meditative or reflective exercise indicated by a ⛰ sign, and a practice suggestion to try out within your ordinary day-to-day life indicated by a ☘ sign. Sometimes there's a suggestion to do some writing and this is indicated by a ✎ sign. I encourage you to do these reflections and exercises as you go along. This will help you not only to get the most out of this book, but to discover on a deeper level how life works. My own teacher, Sangharakshita, cites the old proverb, 'an ounce of practice is worth a ton of theory' – and as Buddhism is primarily about practice I've wanted to guide us in doing, not just reading.

Chapter one

....

Doing it for you

I remember taking my nephew to his swimming lesson when he was three years old. It was a difficult time in his young life; his mother was seriously ill – that's why I was looking after him – and he was prone to being unsettled. I had been nervous about the lesson, but at first all seemed to be going well. Then suddenly he turned against me. Something – I've never to this day found out what – had made him furious with me. He started trying to kick me away from him, but as soon as he was on the verge of breaking free he was forced to grab me again as he couldn't swim and hated his head going under the water. It was a tragic scenario. Sobbing bitterly with rage and frustration, he was literally trying to push me away and hold on to me at the same time, so the two actions were cancelling each other out. Inexperienced as I was with childcare, it was obvious that I had to take control of the situation. I had to get him out of the pool, get him dry and warm, and throughout this, even though he was by now causing pandemonium, stay as calm as I could myself to allow him to calm down.

When we're children, we're not integrated. We have different forces pulling at us; we can't follow a single action through. I remember as a toddler, in some temper or other, deciding to run away from home and cycling as hard as I could on my little tricycle – all the way to the top of the street before remembering there was Swiss roll for tea on Saturdays and turning back. A good parent will hold these extremes for their children and be a steady presence and influence amidst them.

It's similar when someone's drunk. Any teenage girl will know not to trust her friend's big brother when, after a bottle of cheap wine, he tells her he loves her. Even though he might believe he means it sincerely – at the time. Someone drunk can't follow things through; you can't take what they say seriously. They can't really handle themselves. In this way they're a bit like a child too. With luck, they have some more clear-headed friends around who can act as their conscience, take their car keys away, or bring them in out of the cold.

Integration

Becoming integrated means growing up, learning to be more adult, becoming more clear-headed in relation to yourself, learning to handle yourself. It means getting all your energies and different parts of yourself working in the same direction. It means being able to follow things through. And, in particular, it means learning that your actions have an effect in the world.

Another of my nephews was born and has lived all his life in France. His mother is Scottish and speaks to him in English; his father is French and speaks to him in French. By his fourth birthday he could understand English perfectly and speak it if you asked him to, but he naturally spoke in French. Around that time he came to Scotland for a family party. There were lots of kids his age playing in the garden, but my nephew was slightly apart in the midst of them, wandering around with a little frown. The other children were speaking to him in English, which he could understand perfectly, but he was answering them in French, which they couldn't understand at all. A few weeks later he impressed the family – obviously having pondered the matter – by announcing decisively, 'When I come to Scotland again I will speak English.' He'd made the connection. He'd realized that he himself was an agent in the baffling mystery that had gone on at the party. He'd made a significant step in awareness of himself as an agent in the world. He'd realized that the world wasn't just a perplexing series of events whirling around him, sometimes benign, sometimes difficult. He'd realized that he himself was part of the world and that he himself could have an influence in it.

And this process of growing up enough to realize that we ourselves are agents in the world is of greater significance than just being able to communicate with others, for example – important though that is. In fact it forms the foundation principle of Buddhist ethics and therefore of Buddhist practice.

At the Buddhist Centre, I rarely talk about ethics without inviting people to do a simple exercise first, so that they get an actual experience

Not About Being Good

for themselves of this principle rather than it just being something I'm telling them – see the exercise below, 'Reflection: actions and consequences'. I find this really helps people understand any Buddhist teachings that follow in a more meaningful way.

So it would be really good if you actually did this exercise before reading any more – even if you already know a lot about Buddhist teachings. It's probably best if you read through all the steps first and then try it. You'll need a pen and a notebook or paper too.

Reflection: actions and consequences

Sit quietly, close your eyes, and spend one minute on each of these stages.

- Bring to mind, as vividly as you can, something mean or unkind you've done recently.
- Tune in to how this makes you feel physically.
- Tune in to how it makes you feel about yourself.
- Tune in to how it makes you feel in relation to the world at large.
- Open your eyes and write three or four words about how you felt physically, three or four words about how you felt about yourself, three or four words about how you felt in relation to the world at large.

Now close your eyes again and bring to mind, as vividly as you can, something kind or generous you've done recently, no matter how small. Again, spend one minute on each of these stages.

- Tune in to how this makes you feel physically.
- Tune in to how it makes you feel about yourself.
- Tune in to how it makes you feel in relation to the world at large.
- Open your eyes and write three or four words about how you felt physically, three or four words about how you felt about yourself, three or four words about how you felt in relation to the world at large.

Now just sit quietly for another minute to absorb the experience.

When they do this exercise at the Buddhist Centre, most people report that bringing to mind their unkind action makes them feel physically tense and contracted, ashamed of themselves, and fearful and isolated in relation to the world. Bringing to mind their kind or helpful action, by contrast, makes them feel physically warm, proud of themselves, and 'rightfully on the earth' and connected with the world at large.

I often think that, if only I reflected like this every day after meditation, or every night before I went to sleep, I'd become quite a different person. This is because the reflection gives me a direct experience of the relationship between my actions and their consequences. It helps to teach me that my actions always have repercussions, whether I'm conscious of that or not. It helps to teach me that my actions aren't detachable from me. They are part of me and they are modifying me, changing me, all the time, because I'm doing things all the time. I can see that deepening awareness of myself as an ethical agent, as someone who has an effect, would lead me, quite naturally, to take more responsibility for my actions.

If you act as though your actions can be detached from you, when they are actually part of you, you are setting up forces of conflict and disintegration within yourself. My friend Canute, mentioned in the Introduction, said that the more he meditated the more he recognized that getting drunk and then getting into fights was having a bigger negative effect on him than he'd previously realized. The increased awareness he was gaining from meditation made him realize that his behaviour was putting him in all kinds of states of mind that were painful in themselves and at the same time actively working against what he really wanted. He increasingly felt the unsatisfactoriness, even the agony, of that. He made some changes but he was still addicted to the nightlife and all that went with it. The climax came when he got into a really serious fight and lost his licence to be a doorman. Out of work, he had time to reflect. He realized he couldn't continue to meditate and change his inner state without more radically changing how he was acting on the outside. It was a critical moment in his spiritual development. He had to make some decisive changes – such as giving up working in the nightclubs altogether – to bring the one more into line with the other. This realization and the steps he took as a result marked a critical moment in his spiritual development. From that moment, he says, 'I gradually started growing into a whole person rather than a person of two paths.'

Canute's life story is fairly dramatic. Perhaps yours is less so. But you too probably find yourself as 'a person of two paths' – or more – to a greater or lesser extent. Maybe you can easily give presentations at work but find yourself overcome by shyness at your art class. Or maybe you treat your mother as just someone to do your washing, but are the height of chivalry with your girlfriend. Or maybe you never swear when you're at a place like the Buddhist Centre but swearing is the natural mode with the friends you go to the pub with. But then one day your pub friends come to the Buddhist Centre, or you go to dinner with your mum and your girlfriend, or someone from work joins your art class and you don't quite know which one of your selves to be. One of the reasons many people can often feel a bit nervous before these encounters is that their multiple selves will be exposed.

I remember something that happened to me once, which highlighted this area. A young student had come to the Buddhist Centre and asked if she could interview me about Buddhism for her project. I can't remember what I said but no doubt I spoke eloquently about the principles of Buddhism and I do remember my glow of satisfaction as she shook my hand at the end and thanked me profusely. A few weeks later I was in a department store and I noticed I'd been overcharged and pointed this out. I was redirected to customer service, for which there was a slow-moving queue. By the time I reached the front I was filled with exasperation, which, I'm ashamed to say, resulted in me speaking irritably and in raised tones to the customer-service lady. Suddenly I heard a shy 'Hello' behind me. It took me a moment to recognize the speaker, but when I did I blushed with shame as I realized it was the young student who'd interviewed me. I was well and truly caught out. There I'd been, talking about Buddhism in the comfort of the Buddhist Centre. And here I was in the store, acting quite differently, believing I could take 'time out' from being a Buddhist, proving how far I was from being a whole person who has brought her actions into line with her deeper values.

Canute's story also illustrates that the more awareness you bring to the fact that your actions cannot be detached from you, that they're having an effect on you all the time, the more painfully you'll experience the dissonance between how you know you'd like to act and how you actually do act. This in turn will tend to make you feel impelled to bring your actions into line with your deeper values.

But his story also illustrates that waiting for change to happen naturally might not be enough. If you want to grow and develop, you will have to take action to help yourself become more and more of a complete person. In other words, you will have to actively work at becoming more integrated. Otherwise all the different competing impulses within you will pull against each other, which will not only be painful in itself but will also stop you being able to grow: to the extent that your energies are pulling against each other, you won't be able to commit yourself to any particular course of action. You won't be able to follow your intentions through. In the next section, I'll suggest some specific ways to cultivate more integration.

Taking responsibility

My first suggestion is to practise taking responsibility for your own moods instead of giving in to the tendency of blaming circumstances – or other people.

My French nephew took a significant step into 'grown-upness' by realizing that the world wasn't just something that he was at the mercy of, but that he could make a creative choice that completely transformed his experience. It's the same for us. We too can step into more maturity when we realize that, although we may not have any choice about the events that life presents to us, we always have a choice about how we respond.

This isn't easy. The instinct to blame is very strong. I remember once, when a friend of mine asked how I was, I replied that I'd been fine, really positive in fact, until so-and-so came along and started venting their negativity, and then left – leaving me in a bad mood. 'Well', my friend said, with a roguish twinkle, 'you obviously weren't in as positive a state as you imagined you were, Subhadramati!' He was pointing out that a truly positive state is one that can be sustained whatever life brings along, not one that will disintegrate at the first difficulty. Once I got over the shock (I had been hoping for some sympathy), I realized that I felt surprisingly exhilarated. In fact that exhilaration is still having a ripple effect nearly twenty years later. It wasn't that I hadn't heard this notion of taking responsibility before, but in that moment it entered my mind and heart more deeply. In that moment I realized there was the potential for freedom.

I realized a little more deeply that things that happen to me, whether they are pleasant or painful, whether they've arisen from external circumstances or in my own mind, just are. They've already happened. It's how I respond that's the crucial thing. Whatever happens, even the unpleasant things, there's always the potential to respond skilfully, in other words to maintain positivity. It's true that some circumstances will make this feel very difficult. That's why it's good to start practising 'not blaming' in small matters. And it's important to remember that 'not blaming' someone doesn't mean you have to agree with them, condone their actions or even like them. And it doesn't mean pretending that some experiences are not unpleasant when they are. It simply means taking responsibility for your own mental states. I can experience the unpleasantness of someone complaining to me for twenty minutes, but it doesn't mean I have to be in a bad mood for the rest of the day. That's where the freedom lies. Eventually this practise of not blaming may completely turn around your view of the world. What you may have seen as obstacles to skilful action, to positive states of mind, will become opportunities. This is what the eighth-century Buddhist monk Shantideva was getting at when he said that even an enemy is a help on the Buddhist path, because an enemy is giving you the chance to perfect the virtue of patience![1]

Keeping your word

My next suggestion of a way to cultivate more integration is to practise keeping your word, keeping to what you say you'd do, keeping your side of the bargain. Keeping your word will sometimes test you because you won't be able to give in to your resistances, the parts of you that want an easy life, the parts that don't really want to change. Maybe you promise a friend that you'll help her paint her living room at the weekend. But then another friend offers you a spare ticket for that play you'd been hoping to see – and it's for the very afternoon you'd committed. Or maybe you tell a sick neighbour to let you know if there is anything you can do to help. Then just as you're feeling warmed by the glow of your own altruism, they come back to you and say, 'Actually there is something' – and it turns out to be something you'd much rather not do. Each time you give your word, your level of integration – your ability to follow through – is tested.

We sometimes give our word implicitly too. When I borrow books from the poetry library there's an implicit agreement that I'll take them back by the due date. I'm afraid I'm not very good at this. I love getting new books out and I know, of course, that part of the deal is to bring them back on time. I probably sort of mean to, but once I've got what I wanted that awareness, which is obviously not nearly as developed as the desire, subsides. Losing interest like this is a childish attitude to life. Author and teacher Maitreyabandhu compares it to 'a teenager who litters the pavement after unwrapping a chocolate bar'.[2] In my case I often let the books become overdue and each time I do so I prove my own lack of ability to keep my promises. I prove my own lack of integration.

If breaking your word is a sign of lack of integration, as well as being disintegrating in itself, keeping your word will mature you. You can become integrated by intentionally keeping your word. You could, for example, practise being on time for appointments rather than habitually late. You could follow up on the suggestion you made to meet your workmate for coffee sometime instead of keeping it deliberately vague. You could decide not to pull out of an arrangement to do something because a more tempting offer has come up, or because by the time it comes round you've let yourself get overcommitted.

In Buddhism we often use the image of a lotus flower as a metaphor for spiritual development, our own growth being likened to its petals naturally unfolding. But, when I think of integration, quite a different image comes to mind, one that is less gentle and more forceful. The image I think of is that of a laser beam.

I always loved the lasers in the physics laboratory with their beams of beautiful, pure, scintillating colour – although of course you'd never look at the beam head-on or it would burn right through you. When I saw one for the first time I had never seen anything remotely like

Not About Being Good

Ordinary Light

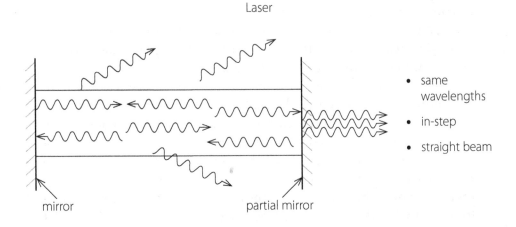

- different wavelengths
- out of step
- diffuse beam

Laser

- same wavelengths
- in-step
- straight beam

mirror   partial mirror

Fig. 1: A model for how awareness and integration work

it before. It was nothing like the ordinary light from a bulb or torch. I like to think that acting with the awareness of ourselves as a moral agent in the world, as opposed to acting without that awareness, is like the difference between laser light and light from an ordinary torch. Lasers are far more than just very good torches. A laser starts off with weak light and keeps adding more and more energy so the light waves become ever more concentrated. The light from an ordinary torch contains lots of different light rays of different wavelengths – that is, different colours – which are incoherent or out of step with one another. But in laser light, all the light rays have the same wavelength, which means they are one pure colour and they are absolutely in step. Because they are in step, they don't cancel each other out in the way the out-of-step light from the torch does. (Or in the way my first little nephew's actions did.) They add together. Not only that, carefully placed mirrors mean that all the light that is emitted moves in the same direction rather than just being scattered about. This is what makes laser light such a powerful concentration of energy. Figure 1 shows how it works.

So you could think of adding more and more ethical awareness to your actions, so they become purer, like the pure colour of a laser beam, more coherent – or integrated – and all go in the same direction. Instead of being weak, diffuse, and all over the place, they would become more and more powerful and potent.

If you work at becoming more integrated, you will begin to feel more self-confidence because you'll be able to rely on yourself. Others will tend to trust you more too because there will be a certain consistency in your behaviour and your attitude. You won't be at the mercy of sentimental emotions or your whims and fancies. Your friends will trust that you won't be subject to liking them one day and disliking them the next. There will be something steady and enduring there to relate to. Years ago, when I was teaching in the Dublin Buddhist Centre, someone realized the benefit to his friendships of being trustworthy in a rather charming way. We'd been debating whether or not one should always be truthful in speech. The conversation was in danger of getting a bit literalistic, even legalistic, when suddenly Matt had a 'light-bulb moment'. 'If I always told the truth,' he said, 'everyone would trust me. I'd be walking down the street and they'd call out "Here comes Matt-who-tells-the-truth!"' I'll never forget how Matt seemed to grow in stature as he imagined this, how he embodied positive pride, freedom, and confidence. I hope he's still there in Dublin, striding down the street, trusted for his consistency in telling the truth!

And just to add, being integrated and reliable doesn't mean that you'll become boringly predictable. A Buddha would be absolutely reliably compassionate, wise, and fearless, but how those qualities manifested would be free and spontaneous. The more integrated you are, the more your ethical awareness will act like a touchstone for you, so the more free and spontaneous this will allow you to be.

Karma

To understand that you are an ethical agent and that your actions have consequences is to understand what Buddhism calls the law of karma.

It's always a popular, and often controversial, topic. On our Saturday open days at the Buddhist Centre, we have taster sessions of meditation, talks, and discussions. Usually several hundred people drop by – for many of them it is their first time inside a Buddhist centre. When we chose the subject of karma for one of the talks, I wasn't surprised to find the shrine-room was packed out. And neither was I surprised when, on asking people what they thought the word 'karma' meant, the top answers were 'fate' and 'destiny'. My laptop thesaurus adds 'chance', 'providence', 'luck', 'fortune', 'coincidence', 'accident', and 'predestination' to these.

People often think that the law of karma is saying that anything bad that happens to you is your own fault. In fact, in Buddhism the Sanskrit 'karma' simply means 'action', or more accurately 'willed or volitional action' (as opposed to involuntary action, such as getting flustered in the company of someone you're attracted to). And karma includes actions of speech and mind, as well as bodily action. The fruit or consequences of action are called karma-vipāka. And the law of karma states that the consequences of a volitional action, that is, of karma, are appropriate to the volitional impulse behind the action.

To understand this properly it's helpful to set it in the context of the Buddha's fundamental insight into the nature of reality.

The Buddha saw that the whole of reality is made up of processes that aren't random, or predestined, but arise and pass away in dependence on a network of conditions. In other words there are natural laws governing the relationships between conditions and their effects, and the Buddha saw that this applies to everything: all the processes in the external world, all the processes in the human mind, and the processes by which he himself, born as a human being, realized the state we call Enlightenment and thus became a Buddha. This is the overall law of conditionality or 'conditioned arising'.

A fifth-century scholar called Buddhaghosa categorized these processes into five different groups, where each group of processes is governed by a natural law or niyama. Sangharakshita in turn has given the teaching of the five niyamas a fuller exposition.[3] He has emphasized its centrality and drawn out the implications implicit in Buddhaghosa's categorization – the most important one being that the Buddha's teaching of conditionality operates at all possible levels.

So we have:

1. the natural laws that govern inorganic matter (for example the law of gravity);
2. the natural laws that govern organic life (for example the process of photosynthesis);
3. the natural laws that govern simple consciousness, including instincts (from the simple: your mouth watering when you smell chips with vinegar; to the more complex: the way penguins find their way home);
4. the natural law that governs the relationship between our intentional actions and the effects of our actions (this is karma-niyama);
5. finally, the natural law that means human beings can become Buddhas (this is Dharma-niyama).

It's these last two that particularly apply to the spiritual life because they concern individual consciousness that's aware of itself. I'll be coming back to Dharma-niyama processes in Chapter 8. For now, I'll continue exploring karma-niyama, the law of karma.

Karma-niyama is the operation on one level of the overall law of conditionality. The law of karma applies wherever there is mind and

Not About Being Good

will. It is the law that governs ethical life. It emphasizes the central importance of your states of mind.

Karma-niyama is saying the universe is structured in such a way that the consequences of a conscious action relate to the volitional impulse behind the action. So if you act skilfully, that is from awareness and unselfish intentions, you will, generally speaking, feel enriched and expanded. You will feel more connected with others and experience pleasant feedback from your environment. And, most importantly, all this will mean you'll be further encouraged in your impulses of awareness and unselfishness. On the other hand, if you act unskilfully, that is from unawareness or selfish intentions, you will, generally speaking, feel impoverished and cramped. You will feel isolated from others, and experience unpleasant feedback from your environment. And, crucially, you will have reinforced the habits of unawareness or selfishness.

So Buddhism has no need for a framework of absolute ethical standards. It has no need for the notions of 'good' and 'bad'. Instead Buddhism asks you to examine your experience deeply, especially to become more aware of the intentions underlying your actions. And it gives you practices and teachings to help you transform your unskilful impulses into skilful ones. It gives you practices to transform your unawareness into awareness, your selfish impulses into generous ones, and your hatred into love and compassion.

There are a number of important implications to draw out from this short description of the law of karma.

First, because there are five niyamas, you can't be sure that whatever happens to you – or anyone else – whether it's good or bad, is because of a skilful or unskilful action in the past. It could have been as a result of any of the five niyamas, or a mixture of them. So my upset tummy could be a result of (a) eating pickles, (b) catching gastric flu, (c) nervous excitement about welcoming a hundred people onto a retreat, (d) regret over getting angry with a friend – or indeed a combination of these things.

Secondly, according to Buddhism, the processes and operations of our minds are themselves actions. So it's not only acting from particular intentions that will make these tendencies grow stronger. Whatever states of mind you allow yourself to dwell in will also strengthen. So, for example, if you keep rehearsing arguments in your mind, the tendencies to anger and irritation will be reinforced. The Buddha said they will etch themselves into your character, like a rock carving.[4] By contrast, dwelling in – as well as acting from – states of generosity and awareness will result in you growing into someone for whom these states become more and more natural.

Thirdly, although every single thing that happens to you can't be said to be necessarily the result of your own actions, at the same time you will tend to create the world that you live in. I'm fond of telling one of Aesop's fables to illustrate this. The story goes that a man is sitting by a crossroads. Presently a grumpy-looking traveller comes by and says to the man, 'Here you – what's the next village like? Are the people honest and friendly?' The man, instead of answering directly, says, 'Tell me about the village you have come from. Were the people there honest and friendly?' 'Not a bit of it,' replies the traveller, 'they were all thieves, liars, and lazy good-for-nothing rogues.' 'Ah,' replied the man, 'I'm sorry to have to tell you that you'll find the next village no better.' And the traveller goes on his grumpy way. Presently another traveller approaches, smiling as he comes, and says, 'Excuse me good sir, can you tell me about the next village? Are the people honest and friendly?' The man asks the same question of the second traveller who replies, 'In the last village everyone was friendly, generous, industrious, and honest.' And the man replies, 'I'm delighted to tell you that you'll find those in the next village exactly the same.' The moral of the fable of course is that both travellers have come from the same village but have experienced it in totally different ways. I think this little tale is saying more than the notion that different people look at the world through differently tinted spectacles. Life is more dynamic than that. We affect the world. You could even say we draw particular people and experiences towards us. A kind of affinity operates. I have a friend who is of a particularly sunny disposition. I am sure he experiences the world as full of smiling, friendly people – he's far too unassuming to realize that everyone has brightened up because he just walked into the room.

Fourthly, the law of karma is part of a *natural* system. The Buddha didn't invent the law of karma – just as Isaac Newton didn't invent the law of gravity. Isaac Newton couldn't have been the first person in history to see an apple fall to the ground! But just as Newton,

Not About Being Good

Practice suggestion: keeping your word

This practice is about following through commitments that you've made. First of all, decide how long you'd like to try this practice for. A week would be a good length of time. Make a note of the 'end time'.

Now decide on the arena of your practice. For example:

- you could decide to be on time for every appointment;
- you could decide not to make arrangements in a vague way, but to be clear;
- if you have a meditation practice you could decide to stick with each session and not walk out on yourself;
- if you've got stuff you've borrowed and should have returned by now you could take it back;
- or there may be another area that feels appropriate for you.

You might want to think of ways to remind yourself of your practice – a note on your fridge or a special screen saver. And it can be good to anticipate any difficulties and how you might work with them.

When you come to the end of the practice period, review how you got on.

- If you managed to do it – what helped?
- If you didn't manage – what would have needed to be in place?
- What were the effects of doing, or attempting to do, the practice?
- Are you going to continue it?
- If so, how long for?

---

endowed with an imagination that was fertile and pliable, was able to see the wealth of implication in what he observed, so was the Buddha, albeit in an infinitely more overarching way. This is not to say that the Buddha was simply a glorified scientist, but to emphasize that the law of karma operates like the laws of gravity or thermodynamics – you can know about it or not, believe in it or not, but it's operating just the same with no need of a 'cosmic overseer', much less a cosmic judge to give rewards and administer punishments.

Sometimes I try to imagine what it would be like if I was as sensitive to the law of karma as I am to the law of gravity.[5] While I'm writing this I'm staying on a Scottish island. Every day I go for a walk or a run along the shore road. There's a drop of about four feet at the side of the pavement – into the water if the tide is in and onto the rocks if it's out. For most of the way there are iron railings guarding the edge, but in one section there aren't any railings and the edge is exposed. I know instinctively not to run on the very edge, that to step off the edge means not to hover in the air like some cartoon character, or to fly, but to fall to land in the water or on the rocks, neither of which I'd enjoy very much. But I don't have to think about that, the knowledge is 'in my bones'. I believe the law of karma intellectually and, to some extent (as a result of reflections such as the one at the beginning of this chapter), I believe it emotionally too. But what if I knew it in my bones as deeply as I know the law of gravity? That knowledge would affect all of my actions. I would see that it wasn't worth it to let resentments fester or indulge in righteous indignation. I wouldn't speak harshly to my friend, no matter how justified I felt I was. And I would see that even the smallest of my actions are not as insignificant as I might have thought. I'd take my library books back on time.

Chapter two

....

Doing it for others

The teaching on karma that we explored in Chapter 1 is expressed poetically in the first two verses of the Dhammapada, or 'Way of Truth', written down in the first century bce from the oral tradition that preserved the Buddha's teaching:

> Experiences are preceded by mind, led by mind and produced by mind. If one speaks or acts with an impure mind, suffering follows even as the cartwheel follows the hoof of the ox (drawing the cart).

> Experiences are preceded by mind, led by mind and produced by mind. If one speaks or acts with a pure mind, happiness follows like a shadow that never departs.[1]

Although some Buddhist teachers think the different similes – the cartwheel as opposed to the shadow – are just incidental, others have elaborated on the differences: the cart, representing the suffering brought about by unskilfulness, is a burden to the ox pulling it, whereas the shadow, representing the happiness brought about by skilfulness, is no weight on the body at all.[2] This resonates with me. The suffering of unskilfulness does feel like something that weighs me down and hampers me, whereas the happiness brought about by skilfulness brings with it a sense of lightness and freedom.

For example, when I receive that letter from the Poetry Library and can tell – without even opening it – that it's a reminder that my books are overdue, I feel ashamed, burdened, and a bit paranoid. I hate the letter in its envelope because I feel it's pointing a horrible accusing finger at me, although actually if I did open it I would see that it's perfectly polite. And when I finally do take the books back I can't quite meet the librarian's eye and the whole experience of my visit to the library is less pleasurable. By contrast, when I return my borrowings on time, aided by my writing the date they're due in my diary at the time of taking them out rather than just greedily making off with them, I feel clear, light, and at ease in the world because I'm free from remorse.

The Buddhist word for freedom from remorse is avippaṭisāra, and the feeling associated with it is pāmojja. Translated as 'delight', pāmojja is characterized by a sense of unity, harmony, and integration.[3] Pāmojja is important because, as humans, we need pleasure. The trouble is that most of our pleasure-seeking is misguided. For a start, it often contains a strongly addictive element – as soon as you've had it, you want some more – but the returns diminish and this will eventually lead to pain. Pāmojja, by contrast, because it is not based in craving, will not lead to pain. The notion of pāmojja (the particular delight of a clear conscience) gives you the possibility of wholesome pleasure. In fact you could see the spiritual journey as a matter of cultivating wholesome pleasures to replace the neurotic ones – that is the ones that are bound up with pain. As a good friend of mine said, a long time ago, 'If we acted on what really makes us happy instead of what we think makes us happy, we'd be Enlightened already.'

For many of us it's unusual to think of ethics and morality as something delightful and joyful. We often associate ethics with restraint, even puritanism and gloom. But pāmojja brings you enrichment and contentment, and contains within it the seeds of its own deepening rather than the more familiar inevitable diminishing. There are other kinds of wholesome pleasure too – being in nature, looking at a beautiful work of art – but, as anyone who's ever looked at a sunset with someone they've just had an argument with will know, without a clear conscience you can't really fully enjoy any other pleasure. And, as I touched on in the Introduction, a disturbed conscience will result in disturbed meditations, in contrast with a clear conscience, which allows meditation to deepen.

Resonating with life

But are becoming more contented and feeling more enriched, or even having deeper meditations, sufficient reasons to practise ethics? If I was teaching at the Buddhist Centre right now, I'm pretty sure someone

Not About Being Good

would have interrupted me already, saying, 'Hang on – surely we don't practise ethics just so that we get to feel happier and more fulfilled? Surely life isn't simply a matter of intelligent selfishness? What about our effect on other people?'

That question touches a paradox – even the paradox – of the spiritual life, which is that the only way to be truly happy is to deeply care about the welfare of others. For example, we talk about joy coming from having a clear conscience. But 'clear conscience' is a metaphor. What you call your 'conscience' isn't really a thing that resides somewhere inside you in various conditions of spotlessness or muckiness. It's more of a sensibility, an ability to resonate and empathize with living beings other than yourself. You could say the life in you has the potential to resonate and empathize with the life in all that lives. This in turn gives rise to a wish for the welfare of others. The more you can free that wish for the welfare of others from self-interest, the more potent it will become, and the more fulfilled you will feel. In other words, paradoxically, you will find that happiness and personal fulfilment are entirely to do with the degree of imaginative identification you can feel towards other living beings.

It's easier to illustrate this by example, so here are two stories. The first is from real life.

On our last winter retreat, a woman told me about a moment of realization. She began by saying she'd never been able to understand why Triratna Buddhism emphasizes vegetarianism. She had been adamant that she was not going to become a vegetarian in order to be a 'good Buddhist', and of course she could reel off examples of eminent Buddhists who are not vegetarian. But then, in meditation, she had a spontaneous vision of a flock of wild geese flying overhead. They were so beautiful and so free. It suddenly seemed appalling to her to diminish such freedom and beauty by shutting those creatures in a cage, then killing them and eating their flesh. Simultaneously she realized that in some way the geese were part of her, and she was part of them. She said, 'I knew that to hurt them would be to hurt myself.' I can still remember the radiance of her expression as she spoke. She had had a glimpse of the deeper truth that the practice of vegetarianism is trying to point to, the truth of the connectedness of all living beings. It was a concrete experience of the fact that, the more you resonate with other living beings as living beings, the more you'll become unable to harm them. It will be more natural to help them, and, in doing so, you yourself will realize your humanity more deeply.

However, if, through a lack of this resonance, you negate the lives of others, you will negate your own humanity – as do certain of the characters in Martin Amis', *God's Dice*. The hero of the story is Bujak, who is endowed with super-human physical strength. He arrives home to find his mother, daughter, and granddaughter all brutally murdered – and the two murderers still on the premises. He could easily kill them but doesn't. 'I had no wish to add to what I found', he says.

> I saw that they weren't human beings at all. They had no idea what human life was. No idea! Terrible mutations, a disgrace to their human moulding.[4]

Here the murderers, by their violent act, have absolutely negated the solidarity of one human being – as a human being – with another. They have become, in Bujak's term, 'mutations' – although in human form – because they are so destitute of the fellow feeling that is part of the nature of being human that they have deprived their fellow human beings of the thing that was most precious to them – their very lives.

Killing may be the most extreme form of violence. But violence can be defined as 'doing to another person, by whatever means, what he does not want us to do to him'.[5] This means you are violent every time you try to assert yourself at the expense of another. The Oxford English Dictionary tells us that being 'inhuman' is being 'destitute of *natural* kindness'.[6] Being truly human then must consist in being able to recognize and act from that sense of natural kindness, that sense of solidarity between one living being and another.

That means that every time you breach that solidarity, you are going against something that is natural to human nature. You are in fact negating your own humanity. In contrast, becoming more deeply human means learning to affirm others. You'll tend to affirm others where you have an imaginative identification with them, and you'll tend to negate others where you lack that.

Not About Being Good

The power mode and the love mode

Sangharakshita uses the terms 'power mode' and 'love mode' to describe these two distinct ways of operating. In learning to become more truly and deeply human, our work is to learn to distinguish between these two modes and to make every effort to switch from the power mode to the love mode in as many different ways as possible. That is to find as many ways as possible to affirm the life in another rather than negate it. This asks for a lot of skill. It may not always be that obvious what relating from the love mode will mean in practice. It certainly doesn't mean always being 'nice' to others, just as affirming others doesn't mean accepting and condoning everything about them. If I am being unreasonably critical of one of my colleagues, my friend will not be acting from the love mode if she colludes with me. Acting from the love mode may mean having the courage to challenge someone. Affirming someone means engaging with their potential. It means supporting their strengths, not colluding with their weaknesses.

And of course life will present us with many complexities. Although the love mode and the power mode are clearly distinct – love isn't power and power isn't love – they may exist side by side since we all do have power, at least in some arenas. But even though you have power in a situation, you can choose not to use it. Or if you do use it you can do so under the overall guidance of the love mode. For instance in an election you have a degree of power, which you can use by voting. If you vote in the way that you feel is the most beneficial, on the whole, you will be using your power under the auspices of your love.

As a rule of thumb, if you are called upon to do something to somebody against their will, you can make sure the power mode stays subordinate to the love mode by using the absolute minimum amount of force. For example, I used to work in a Buddhist-run gift-shop in the rough end of Dublin. Shoplifting was routine. It was clear to me that we had to do everything possible to stop shoplifters, including banning them from the shop. In the first instance, we had a duty to protect the items in the shop – we were stewards of them. But according to Buddhism there is a more overarching responsibility even than this. Traditionally Buddhism says it is the duty of a good king to make sure that the social order mirrors the law of karma in order to support people to practise skilfully and so help them develop spiritually. Taking this on board, we also had a duty to try to support the social order being a moral order.[7] Obviously we had to tread carefully here, not allowing any unskilful means to justify the ends. Asking a woman with three windchimes hidden in her sleeve to pay for them or put them back meant invoking the power mode. But in such instances we tried not to use more force than was necessary. We could bar her from the shop, but we didn't have to be rough with her. We could uphold justice while not invoking hatred or seeking revenge.

Deepening the sense of solidarity between yourself and other people means adopting, even embracing, the love mode more and more. The power mode will tempt you with its lure of quicker results, of getting your own way. To leave people quite free to be themselves and not to take advantage of them, to trust in the possibility of their voluntary cooperation while allowing them the choice not to cooperate – all this is not easy to do. It can seem easier to play on their feelings of guilt, or indebtedness, to subtly – or not so subtly – try to manoeuvre them. But even if you do get your own way by these means, what you will gain will be limited and at the expense of deepening the sense of connectedness between yourself and other living beings and thus becoming more truly human yourself.

Awareness of others

Making the switch from the power mode to the love mode hinges on training yourself to identify imaginatively with others. In Chapter 1 I talked about wanting to deepen my faith in the law of karma until it's as strong as my faith in the law of gravity. By practising imaginative identification with others, day by day, moment by moment, your very centre of gravity will start to change. It will start to become more natural to act in ways that are abundant with kindness rather than destitute of it. The exercise opposite, 'Identifying imaginatively', will take you through step by step.

Reflection: identifying imaginatively

You'll need a pen and paper for this and it will work best if you read all the instructions before you actually do the exercise.

Sit quietly, close your eyes, and bring to mind something that some-one in your life does that annoys you.[8] Perhaps your teenage son scoffs the entire contents of the fridge, your flat-mate lets her milk go sour and stinks the place out, or your husband never cleans the bath after he uses it.

Our tendency is often to think they're doing the thing to annoy us. But, just for this exercise, I'm asking you to put yourself in their shoes.

So first spend two or three minutes imagining, as vividly as you can, that you are them, doing this thing.

Now ask yourself (still imagining you are them), 'How am I feeling as I'm doing it? What am I thinking?' The more you can suspend your own usual narrative the better this exercise works – you might even find it a relief to temporarily let go of your own story or version of events.

Now spend five minutes or so, still inhabiting your 'character', writing about what motivates you to do that particular thing.

Now let go of the person you are imagining and read through what you've written. How do you feel reading it? And how do you feel about them doing that particular action now?

My friend who lives in the west of Ireland is married to a German man. She used to be driven crazy by his fondness for playing German rock music at full volume, shattering the peace of their tranquil rural abode. Every time this happened she'd find herself inwardly fuming about how inconsiderate he was and how hard-done-by she was in having to put up with him behaving in this way. Then once, while on retreat, she decided to suspend her own story about what was happening and instead put herself in his shoes by writing what she imagined was his story. She found herself writing, 'I left Germany behind because I want to be with Geraldine because I love her so much. But I miss my own country and playing German music means a lot to me. It brings a bit of Germany over to Ireland for me.'

Geraldine said that after writing this her feelings completely transformed. Instead of hating it when he turned on the music she felt like encouraging him to play it more – as much as he wanted. This wasn't some kind of martyrdom. It was as if she had extended the boundaries of herself. What he wanted had genuinely become what she wanted; her will was no longer totally distinct from his will. And the experience of this was expansive and joyful. The effects of this willingness to extend beyond the narrow confines of our habits and assumptions into the worlds of others are described by Santideva:

> All those who suffer in this world do so because of their desire for their own happiness. All those happy in this world are so because of their desire for the happiness of others.[9]

The message then is pretty clear: to become more truly human, we have to cultivate more and more of a resonance with others. Putting it even more simply, to become more truly human we must learn to love others, and to love others we need to be aware of them. In fact love is awareness of another. We can't just be positive *at* people, like Selwyn, one of the characters in Penelope Fitzgerald's novel *The Beginning of Spring*. Selwyn, who has 'become spiritual' and who 'with the terrible aimlessness of the benevolent' is always casting around for a new misfortune, won't be put off from calling round when he hears his colleague Frank's wife has left him. At the end of the visit we see Frank, the abandoned husband, with his head in his hands feeling that 'he could bear anything rather than determined unselfishness.'[10]

Manners

That Buddhist ethics is primarily about being aware of others is highlighted in the way one important Buddhist scholar, Dr Guenther, translates the word sīla, which is the Pali word usually translated as 'ethics'. He translates it as 'ethics and manners'.[11] We can tend to dismiss manners simply as matters of social convention, or as the very 'conventional morality' that the Buddhist teachings are steering us away from. But there is a very positive aspect to manners. We could in fact say that practising manners is an even more refined way of taking into account other people's sensitivities. Practising manners can become the means for your care and consideration of others to be expressed. More poetically, manners can be the lamp that the light of your care and consideration shines through. So even if something doesn't seem ethically significant for you personally (and as long as it isn't actively going against your ethical values), because you want to take into consideration the feelings and the convenience of other people, you may choose to observe certain courtesies.

So, for example, as a committed vegetarian, I will never eat meat even if that causes embarrassment to someone who has offered it to me. Because eating meat would actively go against my ethical values, 'manners' has to come second in this case. But if I'm on a Buddhist pilgrimage in India, I will be more careful to look neat and tidy at holy sites, so as not to shame my Indian Buddhist friends, than when I'm back in grungy Great Britain, where frayed hemlines are fashionable and might even get me a bit of kudos down at the Buddhist Centre. Or, on a more individual level, while I'm quite happy for others to know details of my personal life, others of my friends prefer to be more private. Neither tendency is inherently more or less ethical than the other. However, it's good manners for me to remember my friend's sensitivities and not to put him into a position where he'll suffer embarrassment.

The poet Shelley writes that the 'great secret of morals' is to 'imagine intensely and comprehensively', putting yourself in 'the place of another and of many others' so that their pains and pleasures become your own.[12] Practising like this would mean your ethical attitude became expressed right down to the fine details. As a result of your wish to be really aware of others, you would notice what behaviour might cause offence or inconvenience to them and try to avoid that. Your ethical attitude would shine through those details. This is why the translation of sīla is 'ethics and manners'. As a result of your practice of manners, your consideration and respect for others will deepen and your ethics will become more refined.

Expanding outwards

On 7 July 2005, during the morning rush hour, four separate bombs exploded on London buses and underground trains killing 56 people and injuring 700. A day or two after what came to be known as 'the 7/7 bombings', I remember being at a public talk by a Buddhist speaker. Everyone was in a state of high emotion. The speaker described how he had feared for his own son's life and then his relief that his son was safe. Hearing him talk I was reminded of being at my gran's house when I was about seven. The evening news flashed on with black-and-white footage of the barriers collapsing at Ibrox football stadium in Scotland. Reports were coming in that dozens of fans had been crushed to death. My uncle Pat, gran's son, had been at the match and wasn't home yet – and there were no mobiles in those days. 'If he's dead, he's dead', my gran was saying, putting a brave face on it. But she was obviously relieved, as everyone in my family was, when, after a few fraught hours, he walked, unhurt, through the door. Of course the fact that he was not one of the numbered dead meant that someone else's son or husband or father was. I can't remember how much of a thought we spared for them.

The inclination to be concerned for our own family and friends first and foremost was what the speaker at the public talk was addressing. I remember him asking, 'This tendency to be concerned primarily for your own loved ones – is it good or bad?' He repeated the question, with some vigour, over and over: 'good or bad; good or bad?'

The more I thought about this afterwards, the more I came to the conclusion that the question of whether this tendency is 'good or bad' isn't the real issue. It seems we're 'hardwired' to have the instinct of protection for ourselves and by extension our loved ones, especially our children if we have them. It's what's helped us and our particular lineage of ancestors to survive. The Buddhist word for this is pema, which is usually translated as 'affection' in the sense of ordinary human fellowship. It's a social emotion and, even though it's limited by being conditional, that is by having an aspect of 'give and take' within it, it's positive.[13] It's a good place to start.

The question then becomes, 'With this tendency as your starting point, where do you go from there?' Do you create or try to create a small, safe, inward-looking unit, defending itself against the rest of the world? Or do you, by using your imagination, use this very cherishing of 'you and yours' as a basis for expansion? And can this expansion go beyond the point where you feel there will be any direct reciprocation? In the aftermath of multiple-death disasters, can you, while being glad that your own loved one is safe (this time), feel an imaginative connection and concern for those who were not so lucky? (As you read this book you could reflect that someone else reading it is bound to be in that situation.) Or, if you did lose someone you love in those circumstances, can you extend your empathy to share in the relief of those who were (at least this time) more fortunate?

Although it may seem like a far-off, even far-fetched, dream to imagine that one day we'd care for all beings as our mother, our father, our lover, our child, the teachings of Buddhism are pointing us to the realization that

> It's we who are in a dream when we imagine that only our close
> ties with friends and family are important.[14]

You can start to realize this dream of being able to love more unconditionally in everyday practical ways. A concrete way to expand your circle of empathy is to deliberately do kind actions without anticipating any reward. It's so easy to slip into a sort of bargaining or bookkeeping position. To think, 'I emptied the dishwasher/compost bin/cat-litter tray last time. It's not my turn. It's not fair.' And you may be right. It may not be fair. In which case you'll probably feel that you have every justification in letting the compost bin or whatever overflow in the hope that the guilty party will eventually notice. And from one point of view you are justified. But you might try to look at it another way. When I bring a poem to my poetry workshop I can justify every line, every line break, every word! The trouble is, as my poetry teacher, smiling sweetly, says, 'Just because there's a justification for it, darling, doesn't mean it's good poetry.' Perhaps you could think of your life more as creating poetry than as an exercise in bookkeeping.

Personally speaking, one of the most striking examples I've known of someone who made it her business to be helpful, rather than to be right, and the positive effects of that, happened when I was in a team running a restaurant. It was a Buddhist business and we ran it roughly along the lines of a co-op. Looking back, I see that some of us (myself included) had got into a rather 'me-orientated' mode. I think we called it 'being assertive'. We were all working very hard, all tired, and the more tired we got the more we fortified our defences, each determined not to do a single thing that wasn't 'our' job and jealously looking at the others to make sure they were up to speed. I'm afraid to say some of us got into a rather negative state: we weren't inspired, we snapped at each other, blamed each other, and usually at least one person was off sick. Then a new team member arrived and brought with her quite a different attitude. 'You look tired,' she'd say to someone, 'why don't you take the evening off – I'll work your shift for you.' Or, 'This staffroom could be so much nicer for us all – I'll spend a few of my free days painting it.' It wasn't too long before a change started to take place. We all started looking out for each other more, helping each other, noticing when another was tired, not so we could resent them for it, but so we could offer to help. The whole place became more enjoyable to work in: it felt like being in a field of mutual generosity. And everyone benefited. Instead of having just one person looking out for you (that is, yourself), you had six or seven! Hardly anyone was off sick anymore. We probably all worked even harder – we certainly got more done – but no one was counting. It felt more like play than work. The whole culture had changed.

All this simply wouldn't have happened if the first person hadn't taken the plunge. It was counter-intuitive of course. She couldn't have really known what would happen. She must have done it for its own sake. This showed me that if we can learn to 'love where there is no reason to love',[15] help where there is no reason to help, we will be contributing to creating a better world for all of us.

Compassion

So far in this chapter I've said a lot about imaginatively identifying with others. But what if someone is doing something you're really struggling to understand, that you might even feel you just can't understand? It may be someone who seems to be wilfully causing pain to others, or someone who seems to be hell-bent on their own destruction. This can be particularly painful to witness in the case of someone you love – an anorexic child, an alcoholic parent, a sibling who returns again and again to an abusive relationship. It can be hard to make sense of their behaviour and it can feel like our very love for them makes it all the more painful for us. In situations such as this it helps me to reflect that, from a Buddha's point of view, that is from the point of view of a mind that has complete insight into the fact that suffering is the inevitable result of selfish craving, every single unenlightened being, in their wish for happiness and fulfilment, misguidedly acts in ways that cause suffering to others and themselves. Seeing this tragic state of affairs, the response of a Buddha is an outpouring of compassion. Seeing all living beings caught in an endless cycle of 'doing what they always did, getting what they always got', an Enlightened being will be compelled to help alleviate their suffering while never being overwhelmed by it.

Even if you are not yet Enlightened like the Buddha, you can try to gain a more insightful perspective on human suffering. You can reflect that all unenlightened human beings are afflicted by craving. This is the human predicament. We're all stricken by the same syndrome. Reflecting on this fact can activate compassion for all beings – including yourself. While all the reflection in the world will not make the difficulties of life go away – even a Buddha can't take away someone's suffering, can't prevent their actions having consequences – reflecting like this can be the first step in transforming your own responses to others' behaviour. Reflecting like this can help you transform denial or aversion into love. Reflecting like this can help you transform horrified anxiety or sentimental pity into more genuine compassion. Reflecting like this can stop you simply adding to the problem.

By 'reflection' I don't mean something cool and detached. For this kind of reflection to be effective, it has to have a strong emotional component. Fairly often in Buddhist circles we tell life stories, sometimes illustrating these with family photographs. It can be poignant to see photographs of a young married couple looking proudly at their baby, or of children playing happily with a hosepipe in the garden, and then hear – amidst the love and positivity – about relationships gone wrong, jealousies, revenge, betrayals. Gazing at those photographs I often feel my heart torn by the thought of how devastated that young couple or those children in the photos would be if they could look into the future and see some of the painful twists and turns events would take. I am quite sure they never set out with the intent of hurting each other, hurting those they loved, hurting themselves, but somehow they dug particular grooves for themselves that set the trends of their lives. This is the heartbreak of the human condition. All beings – including ourselves – want to be happy, we all want to be fulfilled, but again and again we do things that cause our own suffering. Reflecting like this is a good antidote to any tendency we might have of sentimentally pitying those 'worse off than ourselves'. If we continue reflecting, we'll see that the only way to really help others is to get ourselves into a position with more perspective than we currently have, to develop more wisdom and compassion. The wish to grow into a person who has the qualities to truly help is expressed in this Tibetan prayer:

> All beings, who are my mother and father, wander in samsara,[16]
> And so with unbearable longing, I cultivate the unbearable longing
> to become a Buddha.

Here again we have the suggestion to start with the natural goodwill we feel for our own family and expand from there. In the Tibetan Buddhist tradition the phrase 'all beings, who are my mother and father' would probably be taken quite literally. With their belief in rebirth, Tibetan Buddhists could believe that over countless aeons every single being actually had been their mother and father. But we can use the phrase 'who are my mother and father' to stand for those we are naturally closest to.

The prayer isn't saying we have to wait until we're Enlightened until we respond. I recently read in a book some advice that said before you concern yourself about other people, you should 'care for yourself', in the same way that when you get on an aeroplane the instructions are, 'In case of an emergency, attend to your own oxygen mask first.' In fact that's not the first time I've heard that same analogy drawn. But love and compassion are not really like finite supplies of oxygen that have been stored in case of an emergency, ready to come out of a mask. Love and compassion aren't predetermined, measurable quantities that you need to have so much of before you are in a fit state to give any away. In his memoir, the poet John Burnside comes to a similar conclusion. Writing about a very dark period of his life, he says he was suspect of that old cliché, 'You can't love others until you learn to love yourself.' He says his experience was something more like:

> you cannot learn to love yourself until you find something in the world to love [...] what we love in ourselves is ourselves loving.[17]

Similarly, we don't get to a place called 'Enlightenment' and then start to help people. Rather it's the ever-increasing unselfish desire to help people that the path to Enlightenment consists in.

 Practice suggestion: reaching out

In the next day or so, do something for someone else where there's nothing obvious in it for you; you could even do it anonymously. Make the effort to take the person in and check, as best you can, that what you choose to do is truly helpful. And do it as wholeheartedly as you can.

Afterwards, review how you got on:

- What effect did your action have on you?
- What effect might it have had on the other person?
- Would you like to continue this practice of reaching out?

Chapter three

....

Doing something that works

So far I've been emphasizing that our ethical life hinges on our ability to imaginatively engage with others. But what if your imagination, on some occasions, won't stretch that far? What if you've woken up with a hangover, or you're desperately jealous of someone, or you're feeling so depressed you can hardly face getting out of bed? Is Buddhism saying you should wait until you are in a 'positive' state before you do anything?

Or what if – as with any art or skill – you've started off your ethical practice with inspiration and enthusiasm and sincerity, but then as you get more serious about it you realize how little you actually know, how much there is to learn. It's like a double-edged sword: the more you know the more you realize there is to know. You become painfully aware of all those aspects and dimensions you were in blissful ignorance of before. You'd have to make a very wilful effort to go back to that ignorance – even if it was possible. But you can't really see what the next step to take is. This can even be accompanied by a sort of despair.

Going back to our cookbook analogy from the Introduction, it's interesting that Edward Brown, author of the Tassajara cookbooks, whom we also met in the Introduction, says that over the years he came to appreciate the value of recipes after originally eschewing them. I imagine that trying out cooking without the recipes first, with all the successes and failures that involved, brought him to this appreciation. He says he realized that the writers of good recipes were saying, 'Hey, here's something that works, something you could try, something you could build on.'[1] He realized that following recipes can expand your repertoire of possibilities and, by learning from those who've gone before you, you can grow as a cook.

....

In the Buddhist community where I live, if it's my turn to cook and I'm not feeling enthused, or if the ingredients themselves don't look promising – maybe all we have left is a load of turnips – I'll get down a cookbook. I'll probably choose one that I've tried some recipes from before and know they work, and that usually gets me going. Sometimes I even get inspired.

Or, if I've tasted something good, say my gran's scotch broth or my Italian friend's spaghetti sauce, and thought to myself, 'How did lentils and barley, or a few cans of tomatoes, ever get to taste this good?' I'll ask, 'Hey gran, hey Tony – how did you make that?' Hopefully they'll pass on their recipes even though those recipes might never have come from, or been written down in, a book. What's more, because I've tasted their versions I've got a standard I know I'm trying to get to. So, although I'll never make soup quite like my gran's or sugo like Tony's, the effort of trying and tasting will in itself teach me to be a better cook.

I happen to enjoy cooking. If you don't I'm hoping you can substitute another craft or skill in its place. If you think about it, you'll probably realize that there are many things you've learnt, many things you've been taught, and often these skills have been handed down over many generations and have come with guiding principles or instructions that your teachers have (formally or informally) imparted to you. The reflection on p.48 will help get you in touch with that.

One of my earliest memories is of being taught to knit by my mother when I was four years old. I can still feel the texture and see the pale green colour of the wool that I was making into a scarf for my doll. I remember the way my mother showed me how to hold the needles and then how to make a stitch. And then how she handed the needles to me to let me try it out while she watched. At times I'd get frustrated, but she kept encouraging me and would patiently go back through each step with me. Sometimes I'd mess it up and she would unravel and repair it for me. Eventually I could knit without her watching, although for a while I would still go back to her if I got stuck. Finally, I remember the pleasure of surprising her with something I'd made all by myself.

Reflection: learning from a teacher

You'll need a pen and paper for this and it will work best if you read all the instructions before you actually do the exercise.

Sit quietly, close your eyes, and bring to mind an art or skill that you've learnt from someone you regard as a 'good teacher'. (If you don't think you had any good teachers, just lower your standards a little. For example, if you're reading this, someone must have imparted the phenomenal skill of literacy to you at some point.)

Now spend one minute reflecting on each of the following questions:

- Were there any rules or guidelines that had to be followed in learning this skill?
- How did your teacher impart these to you?
- Were there any special qualities about this teacher that helped you to learn from them?
- Did the benefits of learning from them extend beyond the particular art or skill they were teaching?

Now open your eyes and write a sentence or two in relation to each of the questions.

Now read through what you've written. Has the exercise stimulated any further reflections?

What would the Buddha do?

Learning from a teacher can help you keep in touch with, or reconnect with, your inspiration. It can also enthuse you to reach a higher standard. Buddhism, acknowledging the fact that you won't always be able to rely on your own wisdom and inspiration to guide your actions, and that you'll naturally seek to go further than your present standards, has what it calls the precepts, or training principles, to offer. The precepts come in various lists and I'm going to introduce two lists: the five precepts and the ten precepts. Because the way in which you approach the precepts is so important, and because approaching them in the wrong way can be so disastrous (and I use that word advisedly), I'm going to spend the rest of this chapter looking at how to approach them and then introduce the precepts themselves in Chapter 4.

What Buddhists call the practice of ethics is simply the way a Buddha would naturally act. What Buddhists call the precepts is an attempt to write down the principles that we can draw from a Buddha's actions. It's as if the Buddha, by giving us the precepts, is saying to us, 'Here's something that works, something you could try, something you could build on.' So the precepts aren't rules, but principles drawn from the way a being with panoramic wisdom who was suffused with compassion and who had unlimited energy would naturally act. The precepts are training principles, voluntarily taken on by individuals in the faith that they'll be like a good teacher, like someone who's trying to help us to be the best we can be.

'Ethics' then are the way an Enlightened being would naturally act and we're fortunate to have stories from the life of the historical Buddha that have been handed down throughout the ages to show us some examples of those actions. I'm going to tell a few of those stories now. They're the most well-known stories and probably the most well loved, so you might have heard or read them before. Even so, like all good stories, they're worth reading again.

First there's the story of Angulimala. Angulimala was a bandit and murderer – what these days we'd call a serial killer. His name, which means 'necklace of fingers', came from the fact that he'd chop a finger from each of his victims and string it onto a garland he wore round his neck. And while he was on the loose, all the village people were terrified to go out. One day the Buddha was about to set off walking into the region where Angulimala was known to be. Everybody was beside themselves with concern, warning the Buddha to keep away. But the Buddha didn't heed those warnings. When Angulimala saw the defenceless monk coming towards him, he thought he had a soft target. He started following the Buddha but strangely, although the Buddha was walking at a normal pace, Angulimala couldn't catch up with him. Enraged he called, 'Stop monk! Stop!' at which the Buddha turned round and said calmly, 'I have stopped, Angulimala. You stop.' Angulimala, knowing that a monk would speak only the truth, asks him how this can be and the Buddha says, 'I have stopped, because I have cast off violence towards all living beings, whereas you are unrestrained towards beings.' Amazed at the Buddha's fearless demeanour and at his words, Angulimala reformed his ways and became a disciple.[2]

Then there's the story of the monk with dysentery. This is set in the rainy season when the community of monks, the Buddha's disciples, would have stopped wandering and set up an encampment of huts. The Buddha was doing his rounds of the huts when he came across a monk, lying sick and in his own excrement. 'What is wrong with you?' asked the Buddha. 'I have dysentery', the monk replied. 'Who is looking after you?' 'No one.' 'Why is that?' 'I am useless to the community now.' The Buddha, together with his attendant Ananda, immediately started to attend to the sick monk, washing him and making him as comfortable as possible. Then the Buddha went round the community to establish what had happened. When he had heard from their own lips that, yes, indeed, they knew there was a sick monk, and no, no one was looking after him, and yes, this was because he was useless to the community, the Buddha took them firmly to task. He reminded them that, as they had all left home to become homeless wanderers, they must act like family to each other.[3]

Then there's the story of Kisagotami. Kisagotami had lost the one thing that was precious to her, that meant everything to her, her baby son. Not only had she lost the baby she loved, but she had lost the status she'd gained by bearing a son, and once again would be at the mercy of her unkind in-laws. In her distress and denial she was carrying the dead child around, asking everyone if they knew of medicine that could cure him. Eventually someone took pity on her and sent her to the Buddha. The Buddha looked at her with compassion and told her, 'I can cure your child if you can do just one thing.' Of course she was ready to agree to anything. 'Bring me a mustard seed,' he said, 'but it must come from a household where no one has died.' Everywhere Kisagotami went, people were willing to give her a mustard seed. But nowhere could she find a household where no one had died. Eventually the message of the Buddha got through to her. This message is that the cause of death may be illness, may be an accident. But the reason for death is not illness or accident. The reason we die is because we are born. No one escapes. Seeing the truth of this and that she hadn't been singled out for suffering, Kisagotami was able to take her child's body to the cremation ground and she became a disciple of the Buddha.[4]

The story of Angulimala is often told to illustrate the Buddha's fearlessness. It also powerfully illustrates the sheer authority of his

Not About Being Good

non-violence. And it gives us a clue as to how they are connected. Fear often makes us defensive. But there was no defensiveness in the Buddha. He could completely and confidently affirm the humanity of Angulimala. In other words he had complete trust in the love mode, so therefore had no need to resort to the power mode. The authority of the Buddha's non-violence stopped Angulimala in his tracks both literally and figuratively. It completely reformed him.

A more subtle point from this story is that the Buddha related to Angulimala as more than simply the label 'mass murderer'. A friend of mine who's done time in prison pointed out this aspect to me. We often fix people with labels, and thus limit them. It's a kind of violence towards them. In a sense, to label someone like that is to steal the fullness of their humanity from them. The Buddha didn't do that. He approached Angulimala with an open, generous attitude.

And the Buddha's generosity is illustrated in the story of the monk with dysentery. Seeing the sick monk, the Buddha first and foremost saw a human being; he deeply resonated with that life and acted to affirm it. It wasn't a consideration to the Buddha whether or not the monk was 'useless' or 'useful'. He simply saw a suffering being and was compelled to act to relieve suffering.

And he was prompt in his action. He wasted no time. He wasn't squeamish. I imagine him saying to Ananda, 'You take his feet and I'll take his head, and we'll clean him up.' What's more, the Buddha was also generous in regard to the other monks. He didn't jump to conclusions. He gave them the benefit of the doubt, deferring judgement until he'd established the truth of the situation. That can be hard to do. It's very easy to quickly construe our own version of events and then gather 'evidence' in support of it, convincing ourselves that we're being 'objective'. The Buddha didn't do that, as he valued truth far too highly. But then when he did establish the truth of the situation he didn't mince his words. He was very firm with his disciples. He admonished them and made sure they knew the consequences of their actions, illustrating that kindness and generosity include not letting people 'off the hook'. There is a time to be firm.

And then in the story of Kisagotami, out of all the stories, the Buddha's extraordinary skill in compassionate communication is revealed. As ever he spoke the truth. But he didn't bludgeon

Kisagotami with the truth. Because of his deep empathy he was able to lead her to the truth and let her discover it for herself.

I'm also struck that these stories do not rely on miracles.[5] In particular the story of Kisagotami contrasts for me with the Bible story of Jesus raising Lazarus from the dead.[6] When I was a little girl, that story always troubled me because I knew Lazarus would have to die again at some point and so his sisters would have their terrible grief in exactly the same fashion all over again. I'm more satisfied and inspired by the dawning of insight in Kisagotami, which meant that she would never view death in the same way again. For me the real 'miracle' is that there is no situation that the Buddha could not find a positive response to. That whoever he met, in whatever state they were in, from murderer, to grief-maddened mother, he always found a creative, helpful, life-affirming response.

These stories give us a glimpse of the way an Enlightened being would naturally act. The precepts are a best attempt to communicate the principles underlying those actions. They aren't so much instructions for what to do as an attempt to communicate what the Buddha was. Practising the precepts means trying to listen for the presence that is communicated through them.

It's hard to remember this. The tendency to literalize is very deep within us. So it's often the case that as soon as we see a list of precepts our mind will tend to reduce them to a set of rules. And as soon as we do that, depending on our temperament, we'll react to those 'rules' by either rebelling against them or conforming to them.

Not about being good

If our tendency is to conform, we might end up – rather than being truly ethical – being 'good' or even 'horribly good', like Bertha in Saki's short story, 'The storyteller'.[7]

In the story an aunt is trying to entertain three children on a long train journey – but it isn't really working. A fellow passenger volunteers a story about a little girl called Bertha who was extraordinarily good. The children's momentarily aroused interest begins at once to wane. Only when the bachelor adds that Bertha was 'horribly good' is there a wave of reaction in favour of the story. We learn that Bertha was so good that she won a medal for obedience, another medal for punctuality, and a third for good behaviour, which she wore pinned to her dress. As a further reward she was allowed to walk in the prince's park. As she was taking her walk and congratulating herself, a ferocious wolf approached. The first thing that it saw was Bertha – her pinafore was so spotlessly white and clean that it could be seen from a great distance. She ran and hid herself in the shrubbery and at first the wolf couldn't find her. But her trembling made the medal for obedience clink against the medals for good behaviour and punctuality. At the giveaway sound, the wolf dashed into the bush, its eyes gleaming with triumph, dragged Bertha out, and devoured her to the last morsel.

For the children the word 'horrible' in connection with goodness had introduced a ring of truth – absent from the aunt's tales – that kept them interested. As to the ending, they were unanimous that it was 'beautiful'. We probably all know – and love to hate – 'Berthas' who wear their 'good deeds' and 'principles' like so many medals: colleagues who make sure that we know how many extra hours they stayed at the office; flat-mates who glare at us because we forgot to recycle our yoghurt carton. The Bodhisattva,[8] by way of contrast, says Sangharakshita, wears his or her ethics 'as lightly as a flower'.[9]

In another part of the story we discover that Bertha was rather sorry to find that there were no flowers in the park because she had promised her aunts – with tears in her eyes – that she would not pick any, so of course it made her feel silly to find that there were none to pick. This is the giveaway. In being 'good', Bertha's main concern was the impression she was making. In other words she was desperate for the approval of others. And if you tend to this kind of 'being good', essentially what's at root is that you need and are emotionally dependent on the approval of the groups or circles to which you belong: your family, workplace, society at large. This means you end up not thinking, feeling, or acting for yourself, but rather conforming to group values – or what you perceive the group values to be.

Of course for most of us the desire for approval, acceptance, and acknowledgement is very strong. The first step in transforming this tendency is to start to notice and own up to it. Often the best way of realizing that we wanted approval or acknowledgement is not getting it! At the beginning of Chapter 1 I mentioned that a few years ago my sister was seriously ill and I spent some months staying with her, her partner, and their two young children, helping out with cooking, taking the kids to school, and so on. Fortunately my sister responded well to treatment. We were sitting at dinner with a few friends when, by way of rejoicing in this, she said, 'There was one big thing that made the most difference.' Immediately my body rose into a more upright position and my lips started to rehearse the shape of the gracious smile I was about to give. 'Drinking plenty of water', my sister continued. I hoped nobody had noticed me priming myself for the compliment, and I was forced to face the fact that my motives hadn't been as pure as I'd thought.

A more subtle version of 'being good' is being what could be called 'pseudo-spiritual', like Madame Péricand in Irène Némirovsky's *Suite Française*, who would emerge from her sick children's rooms 'with a thermometer in her hand as if she were brandishing the crown of martyrdom', and everything about her bearing crying out, 'You will reward your servants on judgement day, kind Jesus!'[10]

If you've ever noticed yourself assuming a martyred air or doing a task resentfully it may well be that you've succumbed to 'pseudo-spirituality'[11] or 'spiritual bypassing'. Basically this comes from an *idea* that you should be generous, kind, and patient. Because of this idea you deny any feelings of ill-will, irritation, desire, or any other impulses that seem opposed to these ideals. This syndrome particularly affects people who are trying to live a spiritual life – in fact you could say it's a particular danger in trying to lead a spiritual life. The pay-off is that you will *feel* very virtuous and holy. But the price you'll pay is that you'll tend to become righteous, critical, joyless, and removed from your own and others' humanity. Others may experience you as patronizing, sanctimonious, and harsh. Not only that but, because your so-called holiness will be at a very superficial level, you probably won't be able to keep it up. Sooner or later there will be an explosion.

If you tend towards being dutiful and have a perfectionist streak, you will probably need to watch out for this particular brand of pseudo-spiritualism. What can happen is that, if you experience a

Not About Being Good

flash of irritation or lust, say, because you think 'I'm trying to be a spiritual person' you can feel ashamed and, as a reaction to that shame, manage to convince yourself that you are not having the experience. But in fact there is no need to do this. This flash – although it has been conditioned by your previous actions[12] – is not active. Simply experiencing it will not reinforce any negative tendencies. Simply experiencing it is ethically neutral. It will only become an issue if you work it up, that is if you dwell upon it and allow it to develop. The practice is to experience the irritation or lust, or whatever, without automatically indulging it or without automatically trying to deny it. This is why cultivating awareness, especially through meditation, is so important. That awareness will help you to keep the initiative and will allow the possibility of something quite new to come into being.

The opposite extreme to the tendency to 'be good' or conform is the tendency to rebel. However, when you are rebelling you are just as emotionally dependent on group opinion as when you are conforming. When you are conforming you aren't thinking, feeling, or acting for yourself, and it's the same when you are rebelling. When you are rebelling you've always got your eye on the group you're reacting to. You can't rebel without a sense of the group you're rebelling against. In fact in order to rebel you *need* the group for your sense of definition.

We will all have a tendency to either conform or rebel, and it can be a useful aspect of getting to know ourselves to see which way we generally tend. Some might even argue that either tendency has its good points – someone I know who thinks of himself as a conformist finds his friends who are rebels both irritating and attractive – as they have no qualms about indulging their pleasures and regard nonconformity highly. They in turn find him inspiring because of his 'discipline' and 'steadiness'. However, to be a truly mature individual you need to rise above both of these tendencies. This isn't so much a question of finding a balance or a happy medium. It's more a matter of learning to really think for yourself and keeping the initiative in your life.

How you respond to a list of precepts will give you a clue as to whether you have found this point of freedom or whether you are still defining yourself as 'in' or 'out' of the group. If you notice yourself getting legalistic in your dialogue about the precepts – whether internal or external – this is a good indication that you are treating them as rules to be conformed to or rebelled against. You may find yourself totting up your behaviour like a balance sheet, saying, 'It's okay if I'm less ethically sensitive *here* because I'm very particular *there*.' Or, 'It's okay if I don't worry about that area of ethics because lots of other people who are more "spiritually advanced" than me don't.' These are sure-fire ways to know that you've slipped into thinking of ethics and the ethical precepts in terms of their 'letter' rather than their spirit, in other words treating them as rules rather than as principles. If you notice that's happened I'd suggest that you return to the reflection on actions and consequences in Chapter 1 (p.17). Reflecting in this way will mature you and help you discover this point of freedom over and above the tendencies of conformism and rebellion. This in turn will give you more genuine confidence rather than a reliance on the approval – or disapproval – of the group to bolster your sense of self.

As I mentioned in the Introduction, when I first heard that the Buddhist precepts weren't rules or commandments issued from an outside agent, but rather training principles that were taken on as an individual choice, I thought, 'How liberating!' But that was followed almost immediately by, 'How challenging!' It's easier to observe a rule mechanically than try to apply a principle. That's because a principle is constantly asking you to apply all of your intelligence and awareness. Principles are infinitely applicable, and the task is to learn to apply these principles to the affairs of everyday life.[13] This is what Buddhism means by becoming more and more ethically skilful. It takes practice and it takes receptivity to those wiser than ourselves. For Buddhists this will mean especially being receptive to the Buddha and his teachings. To help you apply the Buddhist training principles to your life I've drawn the reflections and exercises in this book from my own understanding of the Buddha's teachings. And in Chapter 4, I'll introduce the Buddhist ethical precepts. I encourage you to practise them with all of your awareness, then review your practice with all of your intelligence. The more you can do this, the more you will imbibe the genuine spirit of Buddhist ethical practice.

Finally, it's important to say that, at the same time as noticing any mixed motives, such as desire for approval, it's important not to let those mixed motives paralyze you into non-action. If you wait

Not About Being Good

for pure motives before you act, you'll be in danger of never doing anything. And in any case, as I found in my example of looking after my sister, we find out about our motives *in* the doing – not to mention the fact that our sick sister gets helped and the homeless man gets his pound coin.

Practice suggestion: what would a Buddha do?

Having read some examples of the Buddha's responses in challenging situations, over the next week, the next time you find yourself in a tricky situation, try asking yourself, 'What might the Buddha do here?' Or, if your reflection takes place after the event, try asking yourself, 'What might the Buddha have done?'

Afterwards, ask yourself whether reflecting in this way gave you any new perspectives on the particular situation.

Chapter four

....

A guide for living

The five precepts

I undertake the training principle of abstaining from taking life.
I undertake the training principle of abstaining from taking the
not given.
I undertake the training principle of abstaining from sexual
misconduct.
I undertake the training principle of abstaining from false speech.
I undertake the training principle of abstaining from
intoxication.

With deeds of loving-kindness, I purify my body.
With open-handed generosity, I purify my body.
With stillness, simplicity, and contentment, I purify my body.
With truthful communication, I purify my speech.
With mindfulness, clear and radiant, I purify my mind.

The ten precepts

I undertake the training principle of abstaining from taking life.
I undertake the training principle of abstaining from taking the
not given.
I undertake the training principle of abstaining from sexual
misconduct.
I undertake the training principle of abstaining from false speech.
I undertake the training principle of abstaining from harsh speech.
I undertake the training principle of abstaining from useless
speech.

....

Not About Being Good

I undertake the training principle of abstaining from slanderous
    speech.
I undertake the training principle of abstaining from
    covetousness.
I undertake the training principle of abstaining from animosity.
I undertake the training principle of abstaining from false views.

With deeds of loving-kindness, I purify my body.
With open-handed generosity, I purify my body.
With stillness, simplicity, and contentment, I purify my body.
With truthful communication, I purify my speech.
With words kindly and gracious, I purify my speech.
With utterance helpful and harmonious, I purify my speech.
Abandoning covetousness for tranquillity, I purify my mind.
Changing hatred into compassion, I purify my mind.
Transforming ignorance into wisdom, I purify my mind.

References to the precepts go back to the time of the Buddha and can
be found in the earliest scriptures. For example, we hear of a brahmin
who had assembled hundreds of animals for a bloody sacrifice and
went to the Buddha to ask for the correct way to perform the sacrifice.
The Buddha took the opportunity to teach how practising ethically is
the best 'sacrifice' of all, referring to all the principles that make up
the ten precepts.[1]
    The negative formulation of each precept starts with: 'I undertake
the training principle'. This emphasizes that the precepts are not to
be seen as rules or ends in themselves. Neither are they directives
from any external authority. Instead they are undertakings to be
taken on voluntarily as a way of developing more ethical skill.
The positive formulation of each precept contains the notion of
'purifying'. The source of this is the Buddha's teaching to Cunda
the silversmith, who has been observing the purifying rites of the
brahmins. The Buddha taught Cunda that real purification comes
from observing the ten precepts in their positive form.[2] In the West
we can have a negative association with the word 'purity', perhaps
conflating it with 'puritanical', which has overtones of banning all
sensual pleasures. But purity in the context of ethical behaviour
means 'not mixed with anything extraneous or dissimilar'.[3] So

in the same way that the label 'pure orange juice' means there are no chemicals or additives in the carton, in the ethical arena 'purification' means purification of all selfishness, even self-oriented spiritual ideals.

In the Triratna Buddhist Community the five precepts are recited and practised by everyone, and the ten precepts are ritually taken at ordination – although this doesn't mean that the principles they embody can't be practised before then. And, as founder of this Community, Sangharakshita has always placed a particular emphasis on the positive qualities – that is the qualities of kindness, generosity, and mindfulness – that we, by practising ethics, bring into being. He has recognized that psychologically and spiritually speaking you cannot really thrive on negations. The spiritual life can't be reduced to a whole series of abstentions. You need to feel that there are positive qualities that you are developing. So, since the early days of this Community, Triratna Buddhists have recited the positive formulations of the precepts alongside the negative formulations.[4] The positive formulations were composed by Sangharakshita; those pertaining to the five precepts are based on the five dharmas, which come from the commentarial tradition and are particularly highlighted in Thailand.[5]

Both the set of five precepts and the set of ten precepts are grouped into those involving body, those involving speech, and those involving mind. This highlights that, as we saw in Chapter 1, the law of karma includes actions of speech and mind as well as bodily actions. I'll go through both sets together under these headings (body, speech, and mind). Each heading gives first the principle in its negative formulation, followed by the positive formulation.[6]

Body

The precepts under this heading are the same for both sets.

The principle of abstaining from killing living beings; or love

Killing a living being is, nearly always, doing something that being absolutely does not want you to do to them. So it can only be done by using force – that is by using the power mode, as I introduced in Chapter 2. Exchanging the power mode for the love mode – which is what this precept amounts to – would mean that, as a result of your imaginative identification with others, you wouldn't just abstain from killing them, but would generally act in ways that affirmed their being rather than denied it. Acting in accordance with this precept, which underpins all the others, means giving complete space to the other person and allowing them to be themselves. It means not taking advantage of others because you have more knowledge or experience. It means not trying to force or manoeuvre the situation. It means trying to generate a response of loving-kindness that will remain undisturbed whoever we meet and whatever state they are in; a response of loving-kindness that will be undisturbed by whether or not we agree with the person or even like them.

All of the other precepts relating to actions of body and speech flow out of the first precept and show its particular implications in different arenas.

The principle of abstaining from taking the not given; or generosity

If you are operating from the love mode, it follows that you won't take anything from anyone that they aren't willing to give. No matter how much you might try to convince yourself that they ought to give it to you, you can only take it by using the power mode. This precept implies more than simply 'not stealing'. Training under this precept means not taking something that doesn't belong to you without being really sure that the owner is offering it.

In the first instance, this means not taking someone's personal property. But it can also include taking time and energy, as when someone launches into a long account without really checking if the other person has time to listen, or indeed even wants to listen. If you do this it's usually because you are so intoxicated by what you want to say that you don't have sufficient awareness of the other person, and what effect you're having on them. It's basically a selfish attitude of putting yourself first.

Of course lots of people, while they wouldn't physically take something, still end up taking in lots of ways: dodging fares, using friends' membership cards, fiddling tax. It takes more imagination to see how this matters. Perhaps if you can't see how it affects others, a first step is to consider how it affects yourself. All of these things involve some sort of concealment and that's always going to have an effect. It will create a subtle sense of not being able to be completely open, not having the confidence that comes from knowing that you've got nothing to hide. Of course some of these ways of taking the not given are commonplace, so it can take courage and individuality to not partake when others around you might not see it as a problem, and may even be annoyed at you for not joining in.

The exact opposite of taking the not given is generosity. Open-handed generosity or dāna is the basic Buddhist virtue because it so completely and actively goes against selfishness. And, as with taking the not given, generosity includes, but goes beyond, material possessions. You can give your time and your energy. You can give your skills. You can give encouragement.

Most of the world today is run along consumerist lines. You get what you pay for. We're used to sizing up articles and services and deciding what they're worth – and we love getting a bargain. You could argue that this is a fair enough way to run things as it encourages an entrepreneurial spirit. But the trouble is that, if that's the only way you operate, you're in danger of ending up with a utilitarian approach to life. You're in danger of seeing life only in terms of quantities that can be bought rather than in terms of qualities that are priceless.

The principle of generosity goes against this consumerist, acquisitive, culture. It encourages more of a bountiful, abundant spirit – as I described in my example in Chapter 2 of the new team member who, by her generous approach, revolutionized the attitude of a whole team of people. I like to think of the practice of generosity as a revolutionary, even anarchist, practice. In the Buddhist restaurant where I worked, every year on the most important Buddhist festival day marking the Enlightenment of the Buddha, we'd replace the till with a big vase of flowers, and invite people to 'eat what they wanted and give what they liked'. When we announced what we were going to do the first year, the local London East Enders were sceptical. 'People will take you for a ride', they said. But people didn't. It was delightful to freely offer meals and cakes, and at the end of that day we counted up more money than we would have done on a normal day. The highlight for me was a few days later. A regular customer came in and, after paying for her meal, handed me an extra five-pound note (about the cost of dinner and cake in those days). 'I couldn't come on your special day', she said, 'but I thought it was a brilliant idea so I wanted to contribute' – a lovely example of someone giving just for the sake of giving, with no thought of return.

Taking the attitude of generosity onto a deeper level, Kahlil Gibran says:

> All you have shall someday be given;
> Therefore give now, that the season of giving may be yours and not your inheritors'.[7]

Sometimes reflecting on your mortality can free you to be more generous. A friend of mine was writing her will and had decided to bequeath some money to the Buddhist Centre to help develop a particular aspect of it. Suddenly she thought, 'Why don't I just give the money now, while I'm alive?!'

It doesn't take much reflection to realize that everything you think of as 'yours' and in some cases jealously guard and protect, will, in the not-to-distant future belong to someone else – if it is not discarded altogether. Another friend's mother recently died and he had been sorting through her belongings. He was able to take his time over this, and he noticed that gradually each object 'returned to itself'. It was no longer identified with his mother; it was no longer a part of her. There was just a vase; just some writing on paper in a language that he and his sister couldn't read. In his elegy to a poet friend, Don Paterson says that death came and

> gently drew a knife across the threads
> that tied your keepsakes to the things they kept.[8]

If you reflect in this way you will see that the practice of generosity is a wisdom practice, because it's aligning you with the real truth of things: what you think of as yours, as part of your identity, is only temporary. As Santideva says:

Abandonment of all is Enlightenment and Enlightenment is my heart's goal. If I must give up everything, better it be given to sentient beings.[9]

Try the reflection on letting go, opposite.

Gratitude

As well as the practice of giving I want to talk about the practices of receiving and expressing gratitude for what you've received. Somehow it's not always easy to receive, whether that's material aid, someone offering you their seat on the underground, or just a simple compliment. But if you don't receive, then you're not allowing others to be generous. In fact, receiving well is itself a kind of generosity.

I have a couple of friends to whom I particularly love giving gifts. However small the gift, they receive it like I'd given them the Crown Jewels. They take great care in the unwrapping, and look at and handle whatever's inside with obvious pleasure. It's a delight when people show appreciation for gifts given and express their gratitude. It's even more delightful when people do that with things that aren't even special presents. I remember when Sangharakshita lived at the London Buddhist Centre. Those of us working in the restaurant attached to the Centre used to make his lunch and take it up to him in his small flat every day. Without fail he received his lunch as though he was being offered some gourmet banquet instead of the simple bowl of lentil soup that it was. He would have had 'every right' to take it for granted that we would bring him lunch – after all, he had founded the whole Buddhist movement that the restaurant was part of. We wouldn't have been there without him. But he never did take it as his due. He was always courteously and appropriately thankful, and from time to time would send us a little card, expressing his gratitude and appreciation. I always felt that this was such a good example of the fact that you never go beyond the need to express gratitude. In fact it's the opposite. The more practised you become in the art of living in the love mode, the more gratitude you will naturally express. Try this for yourself with the practice suggestion opposite, 'Receiving gifts and expressing gratitude'.

Not About Being Good

Reflection: letting go[10]

Sit quietly, close your eyes and spend a few moments tuning into your physical sensations, your weight on the cushions or chair, your body breathing.

If you're in your own room, connect with the fact that you're surrounded by things you've chosen for their use and because you find them pleasing to look at. If you're elsewhere, imagine yourself in your own room.

Now tune into the fact that, to an extent, these are the things that somehow define you as *you* – whether that's as a person who loves books, or art, or soft toys, or gadgets.

Now reflect that one day, after you've died, this collection of things will be broken up. All these things will go elsewhere, to other people. Who would you like to have them? Without getting too caught up in the specifics, imagine other people taking pleasure in them.

How does it feel to be reflecting like this?

Now ask yourself, is there one thing of yours that you'd like to give to someone now? If there is, then imagine doing that now.

Again, how does this feel?

Then gradually let go of this reflection and just sit quietly for a few minutes to absorb the experience, then open your eyes.

Over the next few days you can decide whether you want to follow through on the action of giving something away.

Practice suggestion: receiving gifts and expressing gratitude

Over the next week or so, practise graciously receiving anything that you are offered – whether that is a compliment on your new jumper, a seat on the Tube, a material gift, practical help.

The practice here is to try to allow yourself to receive as fully as possible. A simple way to do this is to meet the eye of the person who is offering to you and simply say, 'Thank you'. If you don't think that anyone is giving you anything, lower your expectations. Thank the waitress who serves your cappuccino, the bus driver.

The principle of abstaining from sexual misconduct; or stillness, simplicity, and contentment

In my work at the Buddhist Centre, I have many in-depth conversations about the precepts with people (women in particular) who want to deepen their commitment to Buddhist practice.

We go through the five precepts together and when we get to this one about undertaking to abstain from sexual misconduct they often say something like, 'Oh yeah, no worries there.' This can be accompanied by a rueful sigh that seems to communicate, 'Chance would be a fine thing.' I get the sense they imagine that 'sexual misconduct' would mean that their life was a string of passionate love affairs. However, from a Buddhist point of view, a string of passionate love affairs does not necessarily constitute sexual misconduct. I've never forgotten the speaker in one of the earliest talks that I heard on the five precepts saying, 'It could be more skilful to be healthily promiscuous than neurotically celibate.' Perhaps she was being deliberately provocative, but the point is that this precept is not concerned so much with what you do sexually with whom, and how often – or not – you do it. This precept is not commenting on whether you're gay or straight, married or single. In fact there's no equivalent to a 'church wedding' in Buddhism – marriage or monogamy aren't seen in themselves as particularly sacred or spiritual. The important thing in practising this precept is to examine the quality of the human relationships and to keep trying to move away from the power mode and towards the love mode.

Sometimes I've wondered why the area of sex and sexual relationships gets a precept 'all to itself' and why it's not simply included in the first precept. After all, Buddhism, unlike some of the dominant forms of Christianity, does not see the sex drive as the very thing that created human sinfulness, 'the very vehicle that transmits the virus of sin through history'.[11] I've come to the conclusion that the area of sexual behaviour may have its own precept for two reasons: first, because the force of sexual and romantic feeling can be so strong, and, secondly, because we have the potential to hurt people so deeply in the area of sex and romantic love.

I remember seeing a cartoon of a woman posting a letter with the words, 'That's it, it's irrevocable now.' The next frame shows her with the postman as she makes him search through the contents of his sack, and the caption reads, 'It's the one in the green envelope...' The strength of feelings often involved in sexual and romantic relationships can mean that otherwise seemingly integrated people can be knocked off balance in this arena. You'll know this if you've ever counselled anyone in relationship difficulties. You can spend hours talking with them and they swear that it's final now; they're going to leave him/her. Then you see them a few days later and you know immediately by their sheepish look that all their resolutions flew out of the window overnight. It's hard to know yourself well in this area because the forces involved can be so unconscious. So it's as well to take this into account and take even greater ethical care when under the sway of sexual desire or romantic longing. In fact when under the sway of these strong desires, you need to be extra careful in relation to all the precepts. It's easy to be led from breaking this precept – say by sending a sneaky text – into breaking some of the other precepts too – for example by then being evasive with your partner.

The reason for exercising this care is that there is the potential to cause such great hurt and distress in the sexual arena. It's easy to underestimate – or ignore – this. And of course this precept doesn't leave out the harm you can cause yourself in the area of sex and romance. Within a relationship, sometimes you can end up compromising yourself to quite a damaging degree. Perhaps you fear that to challenge things might result in losing the relationship altogether and you either don't want that, or think you don't because of the messages society gives. This can have an undermining effect and lead to resentments building up. This is not to say that you may not actively choose to practise 'meeting half-way' sometimes, especially if you have children, for the overall good of the situation.

The positive aspect of this precept is the cultivation of 'stillness, simplicity, and contentment'. In the rest of this section I want to explore how contentment, characterized by stillness and simplicity, is a positive quality in its own right and not simply a middle point that lies between the extremes of crushing out your desires and indulging in them freely.

Discontent in life is often felt most acutely in the arena of romantic and sexual relationships. If you're single, you can dream of finding the perfect partner. If you have a partner, you can wish they were different. Perhaps you think they should be more considerate or more adventurous. Or you might wish you saw a bit more of them – or a bit less. Fantasizing like this, you can easily project yourself forward in time in a two-dimensional way, thinking that, if only these things were to happen, everything would be perfect. The trouble with this approach is that life is not two-dimensional. You bring yourself and all your complexities, even complexes, with you. Practising contentment – which is not at all the same as a gritted-teeth resignation and passivity – will draw you back to reality instead of fantasy, and return the emphasis to yourself rather than the object of your longing. Simply put, contentment comes from loving yourself.

All Triratna Buddhist centres teach the Mettā Bhāvana meditation practice. 'Mettā Bhāvana' means 'the development of (bhāvana) universal loving-kindness or well-wishing (mettā)'. Whether you have learnt this practice or not, mettā, or loving-kindness, is something that can be cultivated all the time – although meditation, by working directly on your mind, will help you to cultivate it most fully. One of the most important things to know about mettā is that it is not so much a feeling as an intention. Specifically, it's an intention of well-wishing. It's active rather than passive. There's a story of a man who goes to his therapist and says, 'I don't love my wife, what shall I do?' 'Love her', says the therapist. 'But I don't love her', he replies frustratedly. 'Then love her', says the therapist. He is pointing out that love is something you do, not simply something you feel – or not. The fact that love or mettā is something you do means that you can cultivate it at any time, however you find yourself, whatever mood you're in. A panel of Buddhists was once asked what the defining characteristic of a Buddhist was. One of the panel said the hallmark of a Buddhist is that they are always happy. But another begged to differ. He pointed out that you can't always be happy – sometimes you may be feeling very sad – but you can always be friendly and well-wishing. So he said that the hallmark of a Buddhist is friendliness, well-wishing, or mettā.

Cultivating the positive quality of contentment will spring from cultivating mettā towards yourself. The meditative reflection opposite, 'Being a friend to yourself', will help you to do this.

Not About Being Good

Meditation: being a friend to yourself

Sit comfortably, in an upright position with your eyes closed. Connect with a sense of your weight dropping down into the floor and into the cushions or chair.

Now tune in to the natural flow of your breath, just following that with your attention.

Now tune into how you're feeling right at the moment. You could ask yourself, as if you were your own good friend asking, 'How am I right now?' then wait for a response. Whatever the response is, whether you're feeling something pleasurable, painful, or in between, whether your feelings are strong or subtle, or even if you don't really know what you're feeling, practise responding to yourself as if you were your own good friend responding. This might take the form of silent words to yourself, such as 'May I be happy, may I be well, may I make progress.'

Continue sitting for five minutes actively responding to yourself as if you were your own friend.

Then relax your efforts and just sit quietly for a minute to absorb the effects of this meditation.

I find thinking in terms of being a good friend to myself both inside and outside meditation very effective in cultivating mettā for myself. A particularly potent method of doing this is to notice how I talk to myself about myself. For a short time I worked for an organization that taught meditation online. My students would keep a record of how they got on in their daily meditations and e-mail it to me for comments. One of the main things I noticed – probably seeing it in writing made it particularly noticeable – was how terribly critical most people were in commenting on their experience. In fact most of my time was spent trying to help people to relate to themselves in a more positive way. However, I discovered that I wasn't always so aware about my own self-critical voice when one day, as I was rushing late to an appointment, I felt a sharp stone in my shoe. 'No time to take that stone out,' my inner voice barked, and then continued, 'it's your own fault for being late in the first place.' I stopped in my tracks. I was doing the very same thing that I was seeing my students

Practice suggestion: talking to yourself

Over the next few days, notice your inner dialogue.

- What do you say to yourself when you do something well?
- What do you say to yourself when you make a mistake?
- How would you respond to your closest friend in each of those instances?

Actively practise talking to yourself as if you were talking to a good friend. Each time you do this ask yourself, 'How does this feel? What effect does it have?'

do. I realized that if I had been walking with my friend and she'd told me that she had a stone in her shoe I wouldn't have responded to her by telling her there was no time to stop. In fact if I'd been walking with my enemy and she'd told me that she had a stone in her shoe I wouldn't have responded like that. Realizing that I wouldn't respond to another person in this harsh way helped me to speak and act more kindly towards myself. I took out the stone and resolved, as a way of cultivating mettā, to practise speaking as kindly to myself as I would to a good friend.

The reason that cultivating mettā for yourself is such an important aspect of cultivating contentment is because, when you don't have mettā for yourself, you are likely to look for love from someone else, especially from a sexual partner, to assuage your sense of inner emptiness and make you feel better – at least for a time. But really that love is something you can only give yourself. And, ironically, to the extent that you're dependent on someone else's love, you can't really care for them; you're seeing them in relation to what you think they can give you. In fact, to the extent that you're using them to compensate for your own feelings of lack, you're looking for more from them than they can actually give you. Trying to arrange the world and the people in it to suit yourself, to suit your own desires, will mean that you'll always be hankering and scheming and yearning. Hankering and scheming and yearning like that will never produce the stillness and simplicity that characterize true contentment. Contentment, or a well-being that you can truly rely on, can never come from external sources, it can only come from your inner resources. And, with care and attention and patient persistence, these inner resources can be cultivated through simple practices such as the one on p.70, 'Talking to yourself'.

Speech

The principle of abstaining from false speech; or truthfulness

Both the five and the ten precepts have this precept in common. Discovering we've been lied to is painful and distressing. Our view of the world and its events is undermined. We don't know what to believe anymore. Acting according to the love mode regarding others means not speaking falsely to them.

However, it's not unusual to feel that, if you told the truth, if you revealed yourself, you'd make yourself vulnerable to attack. In a poem by Norman MacCaig, the poet says he doesn't want to go to sleep by the roadside in case he wakes – like Thomas the Rhymer – with a tongue that could never lie and, if that happened:

> how could I bear
> the triumphant cries
> of my enemies?[12]

But is it really the case that telling the truth will make you more vulnerable, especially to your 'enemies'? Usually we speak falsely to protect or defend ourselves against others' opinion of us. In the last section we looked at the connection between mettā and contentment. Truthful speech and mettā are also closely linked. If you keep cultivating your practice of mettā and ethics in general, you won't be so vulnerable to other people's good or bad opinions of you because you'll have a greater sense of being able to respond positively and creatively whatever comes your way – pleasure or pain, praise or blame. You'll become less fragile and so less defensive. You'll be more robust and confident because you'll be more able to rely on your inner resources.

I remember turning on the TV one day in 1995, in the middle of an interview by Jeremy Isaacs with a man who had greying hair, a beard, an American accent, and who picked up and played a harmonium at the end. I was immediately captivated by his quality of openness and transparency. He talked about madness, about sex, about spiritual practice, and about poetry. He seemed willing to reveal everything about himself, but not in a brash or showy way – he would simply, with good humour, tell the interviewer anything he wanted to know. He wasn't trying to make himself look more colourful than he was by exaggeration or self-deprecation. At the same time I had no sense that I was watching someone who 'needed to confess', someone who 'needed to tell their story' – something that is sometimes confused for openness. I remember thinking, 'That interviewer has absolutely no power over this man because this man has nothing to hide.' 'This man' turned out to be the beat poet and Buddhist practitioner Allen Ginsberg. He seemed totally free, spontaneous, creative, loving. Perhaps, after years of Buddhist practice, he was telling the truth so generously because he had seen that, in the end, there is nothing to defend (see Practice suggestion: what do you hide, and Practice suggestion: the simple truth, on p. 73).[13]

In the set of ten precepts, three more speech precepts are included, making a set of four. First, this emphasizes the importance of speech and reminds us that it really is an action. You really do influence people and affect the world by what you say and how you say it. Secondly, the nature of the additional three precepts points to the fact that skilful speech does not mean just blurting out the truth at every opportunity. The other three speech precepts enhance truthful speech, even temper truthful speech.

The principle of abstaining from harsh speech; or kindly speech

Speaking harshly means giving expression to ill-will through speech. Usually this is because something has annoyed you and you feel compelled to complain about it. Harsh speech might consist of raised voices and expletives, but not necessarily. A quietly spoken snide or sarcastic remark can be just as harsh. Or it might not even be a word at all – 'tutting' or sighing loudly at a group of tourists who are blocking

Reflection: what do you hide?

Sit quietly and comfortably and close your eyes. Tune in to a sense of mettā, of well-wishing, towards yourself.

Now bring to mind something about yourself that you've never told anyone. It might be something in your history, or a view or opinion that you hold.

Now imagine telling someone that thing. How do you feel physically imagining that? How do you feel about yourself? How do you feel in relation to the world?

Then let the reflection go and come back to mettā towards yourself.

If it felt difficult to imagine telling someone what you brought to mind, that's absolutely fine. You can just continue to wish yourself well.

If, however, reflecting like this gave you the urge to confide in someone, you may decide to do so. But first of all read through and reflect on the rest of this section on speech, so that you can include the principles explored.

Practice suggestion: the simple truth

Over the next few days, practise factual accuracy. How does it feel not to exaggerate or distort? For example, if you tend to exaggerate by saying, 'I'm starving' or 'I'm freezing to death', you could practise saying, 'I'm hungry' and 'I'm cold.' Or, if you catch yourself about to say 'My boss is a maniac', you could try to be clearer about what you find difficult – for example, it might be more accurate to say, 'Yesterday my boss made a business proposal that I'm afraid will make my work difficult.'

Remember, as in all these exercises, be honest with *yourself*. The exercises are not about trying to make you feel what you think you ought to feel. Maybe practising like this makes life feel more boring. Or maybe you feel a sense of liberation. Or something else quite different.

the street, or at someone who is moving slowly or clumsily on public transport, conveys ill-will and annoyance very eloquently.

And, as with all the precepts, there's a reciprocal relationship between your states of mind and your actions. I recently heard one Buddhist teacher say that not to swear when you are feeling strongly could be a form of lying and therefore unskilful! I don't agree with this view. I think that swearing will have a coarsening effect on your state of mind, whether it is an expression of 'strong feelings' or just the habitual swearing that can go along with some cultural conditioning. At the same time, the opposite of harsh speech isn't just being 'nice' all the time. Sometimes you do have to offer an opinion contrary to someone else's, or point something out to them, even criticize an aspect of their behaviour. The real skill is to find a way of expressing your argument, even your strong argument, without resorting to harshness.

I remember working on a team running a ten-day retreat. One of the team members had a habit of arriving in a bad mood every day to the team meeting. For ages everyone was too scared to talk to him about the effect he was having. Finally I saw someone taking him aside. The next morning he arrived and announced, 'I had such a brilliant conversation yesterday. I was told what a negative effect my moods were having. Wow! I really hadn't realized. I'll make a big effort to change now. I'm amazed none of you told me before.' I was amazed too. I immediately went to the person who'd given the feedback and asked how she had done it. What struck me was that first she'd worked on her own state of mind. She particularly did this through meditation. She knew that the best chance of communicating with kindly speech rather than with harsh speech would come about by working on her own reactivity first of all, so she was patient. She took a longer-term view. In a situation like that we often don't trust the love mode – if we act at all, we tend to rely on the power mode much more to get something to happen. But this example showed me that, if you come from an attitude of kindness, you can actually communicate much more, much more effectively, because you're more likely to win the other person's trust and cooperation, than if you just resort to harsh speech.

More generally, kindly speech doesn't need to be saved for any particular situation. In Chapter 2, I talked about how loving someone

Practice suggestion: rejoicing in merits

Bring to mind someone you know and like. Choose someone about the same age and the same gender as you (but not someone you're sexually attracted to).

Bring to mind one positive quality of that person or one positive thing they've done, and spend some time reflecting on that.

Now think of someone you know but don't get on with that well – not someone you really hate or fear, as this will be too difficult. It could be someone that you usually get on with but are having a bit of difficulty with right now. Again bring to mind one positive quality of that person or one positive thing they've done, and spend some time reflecting on that.

If it's appropriate, find a way of rejoicing in that quality to one or both people; perhaps verbally or by sending them a card.

Afterwards, take some time to reflect.

- How did thinking about these people in this way make you feel?
- If you expressed your rejoicings, what effect do you think it had on them?
- What effect do you think it had on the world at large?

means being aware of them. Practising kindly speech is your chance to let them know you are aware of them, particularly by rejoicing in the positive qualities you've noticed in them. It can be so easy to get into the habit of criticizing, blaming, complaining, and seeing faults and weaknesses everywhere. Kindly speech is a way of actively working against these tendencies. Rejoicing in someone's qualities and good deeds is like shining a sunbeam on them. You can see them flourish under the light and warmth. Try this for yourself with the practice suggestion above, 'Rejoicing in merits'.

The principle of abstaining from useless speech; or meaningful speech

In a talk he gave in 1984, Sangharakshita said that, whereas the Buddha listed thirty-two kinds of frivolous, idle, useless, or meaningless speech, there were now – thanks to radio, TV, and the press – at least

32,000 kinds of such speech.[14] Of course in 1984 there was no Internet, so no social networking, no widespread use of mobile phones, no piles of free newspapers on buses and at Tube stations. I don't know what that figure would be now. Perhaps it would be 300,000 or even 3 million. And soon even these figures will seem hopelessly 'dated'.

Although we long to dive deeper into the oceans of our minds, we're addicted to the choppy surface. A big contributing factor to that, especially these days, is the amount of input we receive via modern media. Not only do we receive a vast amount of information, we have ended up in a situation where we are always contactable. This too must certainly have an effect on our psyche. Once when I started a new poetry class the leader, as is usual, reminded us to turn off our phones. But what was a little unusual was she said the reason she was asking us to do that was not just to prevent ringtones disturbing the class. She said that by switching our phones off we'd give a message to our inner selves, to our imaginations, that we were going into a different space now – the space of creative activity. By switching off our phones we were promising our imaginations that we would not disturb them with utilitarian demands.

Moving from frivolous speech to meaningful speech is not so much a matter of avoiding or adopting certain topics of conversation. Your speech can only be meaningful, can only have depth, if you allow yourself to access depth, and not fill up every available moment with chatter and 'input'. This might feel uncomfortable. Again on the subject of mobiles, a young woman came on retreat and, as we advise (although not that many people follow the advice), had left her phone at home. She said that she noticed in conversations in the tea breaks, if there was more than a moment's pause, her body would swerve as if to slip out her phone and check her texts. She realized she was uncomfortable with the pause. But it can be in these pauses, whether you're with someone or on your own, that, if you don't rush to fill the space, life can go deeper, become more meaningful. You will be able to become more aware of your own thoughts and feelings, and more aware of other people and the environment around you in a non-possessive, more appreciative way. You will take more delight in the world, which will naturally then express itself in your speech. Try this for yourself with the practice suggestion opposite, 'Reducing input'.

Not About Being Good

Practice suggestion: reducing input

Choose two ways to reduce input over the next week. If you write down your intentions it will help to make them more conscious. For example you could:

- go for a walk without listening to your MP3 player;
- not pick up any free newspapers on the bus or Tube;
- switch off your phone at a certain time – say 10pm;
- not check your social media until after meditation, or after breakfast;
- eat one meal without reading, texting, or listening to the radio at the same time.

At the end of the week review how you got on:

- Did you manage to keep to your decision?
- Was it worthwhile or not?
- Would you like to continue this practice for another week? If so, do you need to make any modifications?

The principle of abstaining from slanderous speech; or harmonious speech

Keeping this precept means avoiding stirring up trouble, making matters worse, and especially avoiding causing discord between people, through gossip, for example.

It's not entirely easy to say why human beings actively cause discord. Perhaps, if we feel animosity towards someone, rather than admit that and take responsibility for it, we create the story that that person is so full of faults that we're justified in our ill-will. Then we involve others to try to provide even more justification. Slanderous or malicious speech can be a way of getting other people on 'our side' against someone else. It can be a way of giving credibility to our own negativity.

However, sometimes it seems we have nothing to gain at all personally. We just seem to get a taste for the suffering or misfortune of others and enjoy it when others quarrel. It can be all too easy to join in with slanderous speech, and hardly even realize you're doing so. It doesn't help that as a society we have created a culture, through newspapers, magazines, and the media, where this sort of slander is the norm, and where gossip can just seem like harmless fun that won't have any effects.

But in fact everything you say does have an effect. You are always influencing others by what you say, one way or the other. Even if you can't immediately see those effects, you can form a clear intention not to get involved in this sort of bad-mouthing, especially where it will contribute to quarrels between others. You may have to use your imagination to motivate yourself to do this. For example, you could imagine that you or someone you love was on the receiving end of such slander or gossip.

At the same time you can actively cultivate the opposite – harmonious or harmonizing speech (see the practice suggestion opposite). You can actively work at creating harmony between people. You can develop the art of taking pleasure in creating harmony. Instead of passing on gossip, you can pass on compliments and rejoicings – they often mean even more when they're passed on than when they're received directly. In this way, you can be part of creating a positive community, even a spiritual community. One Buddhist teacher has said that, in practising harmonious – or harmonizing – speech, 'the tapestry of the Sangha[15] is woven' with 'clean, strong and beautiful' threads (see Practice suggestion: harmonizing speech, p. 79).[16]

These then are the four speech precepts. But before leaving them, there are a couple more considerations in practising skilful communication that I'd like to include.

The first consideration is speaking at the right time. In the *Abhaya Sutta*,[17] the Buddha tells Prince Abhaya how to decide what is and what is not worth saying. For the Buddha to say something, it would have to be both true and beneficial, and he would have a sense of timing for when pleasing and unpleasing things should be said. I like to draw the contents of the sutta up on a chart, as in Figure 2.

We can see that the Buddha would never say anything untrue in any circumstances. Nor would he shy away from saying something that was unpleasant to hear. Sometimes it takes courage to speak. Out of fear of potential conflict we can be reluctant to speak the truth; we can collude. The Buddha would never do that. But, out of consideration

Practice suggestion: harmonizing speech

Over the next week or so, practise abstaining from talking badly about anyone behind their backs or gossiping. A good rule of thumb is not to say anything that you wouldn't want the person themselves to hear. At the same time, if you hear someone complimenting or rejoicing in someone when they're not there, pass it on.

At the end of the week, review your practice:

- Was it difficult or easy to refrain from gossiping?
- What effect did it have?
- Did you manage to pass any compliments on?
- How did that feel?
- What effect did it have on the person you passed the compliment on to?

true?	beneficial?	agreeable?	Buddha speaks?
✗	✗	✗	no
✓	✗	✗	no
✗	✗	✓	no
✓	✗	✓	no
✓	✓	✗	YES at the right time
✓	✓	✓	YES at the right time

Fig. 2: From the Abhaya Sutta: *how a Buddha communicates*

for the listener, he would always make sure that he spoke at the right time. Sometimes, if we're nervous about a conversation we have to have, or if we're just plain busy, we can blurt out what we wanted to say at a time, or in a place, that's inappropriate. That can be painful for the recipient and make it harder for them to be receptive to what we have to say. If you have something sensitive or difficult to say, choose your time and place carefully and make sure the conversation won't be rushed or interrupted.

The second consideration is listening. This too is a vital part of skilful communication. Real listening means at the very least not just waiting until it's your turn to speak – which is often especially tempting if you're having a heated discussion. I remember once, when I was having an ongoing difficulty with someone, I said to a mutual friend, 'I guess she and I will just have to keep talking.' The mutual friend gave me a lesson I've tried not to forget by replying, 'How about instead of talking more you listen more?'

Real listening means trying to be more deeply aware of the person behind the literal words that they are saying. You probably know people who don't really listen to you, and you know how hard it is to open up to them – in fact it can feel impossible to open up to them. By the same token, if you want people to open up to you, if you want to be a good friend to them, you can practise 'deep listening' when you're with them. The first step in this will involve simply taking that person in visually with kindly awareness – how do they look today? Do they seem tired, excited, anxious, or happy? The more they feel your kindly interest and awareness, the more of themselves they'll be inclined to share with you.

I have said a lot now about speech. I've introduced the four speech precepts, timely speech, listening, and I've suggested some practical exercises. At the same time as practising all these things it's important to watch out for the tendency to be so worried about breaking the speech precepts that you never say anything at all – which in fact would be the only way of never breaking them. Sometimes – especially if you're of a temperament that means you tend to hold back in speech out of shyness or fear of conflict – it's best to take the risk and just speak. If you get it wrong it probably won't be the end of the world. You can always apologize and try again.

Not About Being Good

Mind

The principle of abstaining from intoxicants; or mindfulness

These days there are lots of books and courses on mindfulness. People practise it to relieve stress, to help not to relapse into addiction, to help with working with physical pain. But it is included in the five precepts for the particular reason that without it you can't practise any of the other precepts. You need to be aware of yourself, of your effect in the world, and of others in order to be skilful. So this precept is about encouraging activities that support you in cultivating clarity of mind and about moving away from activities that hinder this.

The most direct way to cultivate mindfulness, or clarity of mind, is through meditation. And usually the result of cultivating mindfulness, and experiencing the satisfaction of clearer, brighter states of mind, is that activities that dull the mind tend to fall away. When I first started meditating I was puzzled as to why I seemed to have more money left at the end of the month than before. Then it dawned on me that, without my particularly noticing it, I wasn't spending money on alcohol to nearly the same extent anymore. It wasn't that I'd been a particularly heavy drinker, but looking back I see that through meditation and going on Buddhist retreats my standards for my own states of mind had been raised. I valued the clearer and more subtle awareness that I was now experiencing and I naturally didn't want to corrupt or spoil that. So alcohol-drinking had just naturally fallen away.

Alcohol is an obvious intoxicant. So-called 'recreational drugs' are another obvious one. But there are many ways in which we 'cloud our minds' and dull our awareness: mindless TV watching, shopping, cigarettes. And of course modern technology is constantly providing us with new ways to distract ourselves, such as Internet pornography and gaming.

You might take part in these activities to distract yourself. Maybe you've had enough of the buzzing of worries and anxieties in your head, and you just want to switch off for a bit. That may be fine in moderation but the trouble is that, according to Buddhism, in the same way that eating too much chocolate, or smoking, has a direct effect on your health, the habit of partaking in these more indirect 'intoxicants' doesn't just affect your mind at the time you're partaking in them.

Practice suggestion: looking at how you relax[18]

Here are some suggestions for exchanging activities that tend to cloud and coarsen the mind for activities that clarify and uplift the mind that you could practise over the next week or so.

- Spend one evening reading a classic novel instead of watching TV.
- Bring a volume of poetry to read on the subway or bus instead of a trashy newspaper.
- Instead of having a glass of wine to relax, listen to a meditation CD.
- Instead of surfing the Web in your lunch break, try eating your sandwich mindfully, tasting every bite.
- Walk round the park or side streets instead of walking round the shops.

Fig. 3: The hub of the wheel of life

Not About Being Good

It will have a more general effect on the condition of your mind. I remember going on retreat to a beautiful venue in the Highlands of Scotland, beside a sparkling loch. As a number of us got off the bus into the clear fresh air, a fellow retreatant turned to me and said, 'The problem is that I've forgotten how to stop and enjoy all this.' I took this to mean that she'd filled her life so full of distracting activities that she'd reduced her capacity to simply be aware.

The practice of mindfulness, rather than being simply another way of 'switching off' your mind, is a means of 'going deeper' within your mind. The metaphor of 'going deeper' suggests that you can see your mind as an ocean: the surface may be turbulent and disturbed, but if you can descend below the surface you'll encounter states of mind that are more spacious and richer than you could have imagined beforehand.

One way to cultivate mindfulness is to look at what you do to relax and gradually try to exchange activities that cloud and coarsen your mind for activities that clarify and uplift your mind. This will take effort. It's easy to take the 'path of least resistance' into distraction, so some practice suggestions are given on p.82, 'Looking at how you relax'.

Transforming greed, hatred, and delusion

In the set of ten precepts, the basic precept of mindfulness remains implicit and three more specific 'mind precepts' are introduced. I'll say a little about these in general and then explore them individually.

In Chapter 2 we saw that unenlightened existence is described as an endless repetitive cycle. Buddhism extends this metaphor by saying that this endless round is driven by the trio of greed, hatred, and delusion. In the image of the wheel of life (see Figure 3), these three are depicted as a cock (greed or craving), a snake (hatred), and a pig (ignorance or delusion), and they are shown as each biting the tail of the next, each driving the next forward and on unendingly.

It is with this trio that we are now concerned. Although – to change the metaphor – greed, hatred, and delusion seem to be woven into the very fabric of our being, they are in fact something we do, not just things that happen to us. And if we do them, then we can 'undo' them. I'll look at each in turn to explore how to go about that.

The principle of abstaining from covetousness; or tranquillity

Covetousness is a state where you're reaching out to try to appropriate something external, even incorporate it into yourself. But because this is actually impossible, the state of covetousness is also the painful state of frustration.[19] This is why Buddhism says that it is only by overcoming craving, of which covetousness is an aspect, that you'll be free from frustration and suffering. The Buddha said:

> Whoever in the world overcomes this wretched, adhesive craving,
> so difficult to overcome, his sorrows fall from him like drops of
> water from the lotus leaf.[20]

The image of a drop of water running from a leaf is an image for the absence of adhesion, the absence of stickiness, and as such is the classic image for non-attachment. But 'non-attachment' doesn't always sound particularly attractive. It can have connotations of coldness, even indifference and alienation. I am often asked – and I ask myself too – 'How can I love a person, even love them passionately, without this sticky attachment? How can I care about a cause that I am convinced is for the greater good of all, while at the same time not holding so tightly to it that I feel ill-will towards those who don't support me?' These questions have often seemed like Zen koans to me, in that there doesn't seem to be a logical solution. They are problems that can't be solved on their own level.

The closest I ever got to 'a glimpse of a glimpse' of what it might be like to love without attachment was once when I was on solitary retreat. I'd decided to copy out a long Buddhist text in calligraphy into a book and illustrate every page with small watercolour paintings. I can still see some of those paintings now – a blue lotus, a female swan. I'd also built a shrine with the image of the Buddha to represent my highest ideals, and I was spending a lot of time meditating before this shrine. My idea for the book I was making was that it was to be an offering to the shrine. To complete this action, and show that I wasn't making it to appropriate it for

Not About Being Good

myself, after I'd made the offering I would ritually burn it. As I bent over my work it wasn't long before I made a mistake with one of the letters. Immediately I noticed the thought, 'Well, never mind, what does it matter, it's going to be burnt anyway.' But then another inner voice said, 'No, come on, it's meant to be an offering to your highest ideals, do your best, redo that page.' So I redid that whole page. After an hour or so I made another mistake. Again I talked myself into redoing the whole page. But then gradually over the days and weeks something new happened. I still made mistakes. But I no longer had to talk myself into redoing the page. I just wanted to. The activity had taken on a life of its own. I was simply and happily engaged with wanting it to be the best it could be for its own sake. The fact that it was going to be burnt didn't make me care less about it. And the fact that it was as beautiful as my capabilities allowed did not make me not want to burn it. I offered it to the Buddha. I burnt it in the stove.

You can reflect that everything you make – including your own sense of self – will dissolve or be burnt one day. This is the true nature of yourself and everything you care about, everything you crave or covet. The danger of reflecting on these 'facts of life' is that you might descend into nihilism. You might ask, 'What's the point of even trying then?' This danger was averted in the case of my calligraphy by the fact that I had imaginatively engaged with making the book as an offering to my highest ideals. I remember thinking at the time, 'What would it be like to see my whole life as an offering to my highest ideals, to put my whole life into the service of my highest ideals?' I saw that if I could do this, while being aware of the transitory nature of all things including myself, my priorities would change. It would certainly mean that I wouldn't get into a bad temper when I didn't get what I had been coveting, or when the cause I'd been championing wasn't as widely supported as I thought it should be.

The sort of experience that I had on my retreat is the key to the question of how to love without attachment. In states of craving and attachment you want the object of your desire to meet your need in some way. But non-attachment means the object exists in its own right and not as something to fulfil your need – so you can delight

Reflection: appreciating what you have

Notice what you can see, hear, taste, touch, and smell right now.

Reflect that just the fact of being alive is extraordinary. Even if your life is hard at the moment, at least you have life and awareness.

If you are reading this, it is also likely that you live in an incredibly fortunate place in the world and time in history, a time and place of unprecedented wealth and freedom. Bring to mind all the material things that you benefit from, such as food and shelter.

Ask yourself what else there is in life to be grateful for. There may be your family and friends. Then there are all the cultural riches – schooling, art, books, films, music. There are the teachers that have been helpful to you. Are there other 'blessings' you can think of, anything or anyone that has enriched your life?

Make a list of five of these blessings. If you want to, you can continue making a list of 'five a day', every day.

in it for its own sake. This is tranquillity: a positive, generous mental state where there is no discontent but rather freedom, openness, and spontaneity.

It's easy to focus on what we lack and take the benefits we have for granted. A simple way to cultivate a sense of inner richness and so transform covetousness is to consciously reflect on the positive things that are already in your life. The exercise above, 'Appreciating what you have', will help you do this.

The principle of abstaining from hatred; or compassion

Covetousness is a state where we're reaching out to try to appropriate something external. Hatred arises when we're hindered or obstructed in that, either by the thing itself or person themselves, or by something or someone else. Hatred is the desire to harm what comes between us and the thing, person, or outcome we want.

It can take many forms: irritation, resentment, passive aggression, blame, righteous indignation, rage with other people or even at inanimate objects – I remember seeing someone dash his mobile phone to the ground. It can take the form of pleasure at someone's misfortune, and of course it can be directed towards yourself as well as others, resulting, for example, in chronic low self-esteem. Even reading about the forms of hatred can be painful because the emotions they represent are in direct opposition to human growth and flourishing.

Hatred is a definite desire to do harm – as opposed to anger, which may be used skilfully if, and it's a big if, you have enough mindfulness. The more you dwell in hatred, or even on it, the more fixed and settled it becomes. Once, in a rather misguided exercise, I asked people at a class to call out the forms of hatred while I wrote them on a flip chart and, after about ten minutes, the atmosphere in the room became positively hostile! People stopped simply calling out the words and started to direct them at each other.

Hatred causes our perspective to narrow. Our fixed attitude causes us to interpret the actions of our 'enemy' only in negative terms. They simply can't do anything right – just as someone we're attached to can do no wrong in our eyes. I remember a little incident that highlighted this for me. In the Buddhist community where I live, we meditate together in the mornings. Once someone came in late, after we'd all settled, and started to arrange themselves just behind me. As they rustled about I realized that my emotions were confused. I didn't know whether to feel annoyed or indulgent because, without looking directly around, I couldn't see whether it was someone I wasn't getting on with or someone I was feeling friendly towards. This showed me just how subjective and irrational my feelings of ill-will can be.

It's easy to convince ourselves that our ill-will is justified, especially when the other person actually has done something that has caused us trouble. Once, when I was leading a retreat someone wanted to change the time of supper. I was adamant that it shouldn't be changed and sure I had 'right on my side' because I'd led a similar retreat a number of times. A friend, seeing the state I was getting myself worked up into, told me in no uncertain terms that I needed to calm down immediately. 'Even if I'm right?' I bleated. 'Especially if you're right', he replied. He was reminding

Meditation: changing hatred to compassion

Sit comfortably, in an upright position with your eyes closed. Connect with a sense of your weight dropping down into the floor and into the cushions or chair.

Now tune in to the natural flow of your breath, just following that with your attention.

Now bring to mind someone you know whom you find difficult. To begin with, don't choose someone whom you really hate or who has really hurt you, as this will be too demanding.

- Acknowledge the difficult behaviour and how it makes you feel, and at the same time try to see the bigger picture.
- Reflect that this person too is a human being, like you, who wants to be happy and fulfilled.
- Try wishing them well within your mind by saying, 'May you be happy. May you be well. May you be free from suffering. May you progress.'
- Repeat these phrases four or five times, then come back to the sensations of your breath in your body.

Finally relax your efforts and just sit quietly for a minute to absorb the effects of the meditation.

me that Buddhist wisdom says that, no matter what the other person has done, ill-will is never justified. The Buddha said that 'Not by hatred are hatreds ever pacified [...] They are pacified by love.'[21] He said that this is an 'eternal law', which means it holds true no matter how much someone has upset or hurt you. But the Buddha in saying this is not demanding the impossible. He's saying that nothing will be solved by adding more hatred into the equation.

While you hate someone, you can't imaginatively identify with them. You can't properly relate to them as a human being. Compassion, on the other hand, is a resonance with all beings. It's a recognition of what is held most deeply in common, and the wish to act for the benefit of all. So compassion is the direct opposite or positive counterpart of hatred. At the same time hatred cannot be changed into compassion all at once, especially if someone has hurt you or someone you love very badly. This change will be a process, and meditations such as the one on p.88, 'Changing hatred to compassion', can be a potent part of that process.

The principle of abstaining from false views; or wisdom

What Buddhism calls a false view is not just some sort of intellectual misunderstanding. In Buddhism, what makes a view false is that it's an expression of, or a rationalization of, a state of mind contaminated by covetousness and hatred, as well as by delusion.[22] Not only are false views the product of these unskilful mental states, but they reinforce them, so, unless you take some action, you create an ever more vicious circle. Remember the image of unenlightened existence being like a wheel, driven at the hub by the pig of ignorance, the snake of hatred, and the cock of greed each biting the tail of the next, and remember that unchecked false views will result in the pig growing fatter on the snake, the snake growing fatter on the cock, the cock growing fatter on the pig, and so on. And because – as we saw in Chapters 1 and 2 – all our experience is produced and led by our minds, false views underpin all our unskilful acts of body, speech, and mind.

The Buddha was free from all views.[23] But we can't take a shortcut to that point; we can't take a shortcut to wisdom. At our stage we need first of all to take up 'right views' as a basis for how to act, as a basis for ethics. But 'right views' are not 'right' simply in the sense of being the opposite of false views. Right views are not closed systems of ideas, to be held on to and defended. They're adoption of skilful attitudes taken up as a means to help transform unskilful states of mind. Right views are both the expressions of skilful mental states, and the supports for skilful mental states.

There are many false views listed by the Buddha. All of these will hinder self-transcendence, or the realization of the truth of egolessness, which is the goal of the spiritual life. An early text, the Brahmajāla Sutta enumerates and analyzes sixty-four altogether.[24] However, in abandoning false views we must be careful not to fall into what Sangharakshita has called a 'common misapprehension', which is thinking of

Insight and egolessness in abstract, even metaphysical terms, rather than as comprising concretely-lived attitudes and behaviour'.[25]

Falling into this misapprehension will leave wisdom as far away as ever.

So I'm going to focus on just one example of a false view that we can directly work with in our own experience. It's one of four or five that the Buddha taught to Cunda the silversmith, whom we met earlier in this chapter. The Buddha taught Cunda that it was a false view to hold that 'there is no fruit or ripening of deeds well done or ill done.'[26] In other words, the Buddha said that it is a false view to hold that

> actions do not have consequences and that there is no difference, therefore, between skilful and unskilful actions.[27]

The corresponding right view can be cultivated by practising the kind of reflection on actions and their consequences that I introduced in Chapter 1. Reflecting on the law of karma and deepening your practice of ethics will mean that you continually expand the scope of your care and concern. This in turn will mean that your experience of what you call 'yourself' will become less and less fixed on a single point of identity. The self will increasingly be transcended by 'a creative orientation of becoming'.[28] This self-transcendence is the goal of Buddhism. Realizing it means realizing the truth of egolessness. Realizing it means ignorance has been transformed into wisdom.

Starting to work on the particular wrong view that 'actions do not have consequences' means we can start this transformation of ignorance into wisdom in a very practical way. As Sangharakshita says:

> If we find it difficult to realize the ultimate emptiness of the self, the solution is to try to be a little less selfish. The understanding comes after the experience, not before.[29]

Not About Being Good

Practice suggestion: beyond wrong and right

A sure way to know if you're holding on to a view in a tight, even dogmatic way is if you respond heatedly or get upset when it is challenged or if someone else simply disagrees.

Over the next week, each time you notice yourself holding on to and defending a view or position – whether it's to do with the best way to load the dishwasher, a response to climate change, or something of an existential nature, stop and ask yourself, 'Why does this matter?' Whatever the response is to that question, again ask yourself, 'Why does *that* matter?' Keep asking yourself this – and see where it takes you.

At the end of the week, take some time to reflect on this exercise and make some notes about anything you discovered.

Chapter five

....

A deeper motivation

In Chapter 4 I introduced the ethical precepts in themselves. In this chapter I want to explore how the way we relate to the precepts affects how we practise them.

First I'll look at how the values underpinning our ethical practice affect the way it unfolds. That is, how is the ultimate goal of Buddhism reflected in day-to-day ethical life? Secondly I'll look at how the level of commitment we have to those values fundamentally affects that unfolding.

'What's a heaven for?'

What gives meaning and validity to Buddhist ethics is its conception of Enlightenment. The ideal of Enlightenment is what sustains a Buddhist ethical life. Practising Buddhist ethics is not about just following what other people do. It's not about obeying authority. It's not about aiming at personal happiness or even happiness for yourself and others. Practising Buddhist ethics means living a skilful life as a means of realizing Enlightenment for the benefit of all beings. The ideal of Enlightenment is what makes Buddhist ethics Buddhist. As ideals go, this might seem impossibly far off, and in a way it is – just as my poetry tutor's ideal of being as magnificent a poet as Wordsworth is impossibly high. Yet she still makes the attempt. She has given herself an impossibly high goal on purpose – and she encourages us to do the same. Because she knows that, for any creative endeavour, we need an ideal to draw us on, even to draw us out. And the higher, the more limitless, that ideal, the more it will ask from us. As the poet Robert Browning puts it:

Ah, but a man's reach should exceed his grasp,
Or what's a heaven for?[1]

I once took part in a fundraising appeal where a team of us, over six weeks, walked the streets of Birmingham knocking doors and asking strangers to give money to support social change in India. We had set a collective target, and at the beginning of the sixth week it was clear that I was letting the side down. So I decided to take action. I decided that, whatever the outcome, I wouldn't let myself fail because of fear. So I promised myself and my team that I would take a risk in my communication in every single encounter. I promised not to leave any door thinking, 'If only I hadn't held back.' To prove to myself that I meant it, I pledged to give a donation to the fund myself every time I didn't follow my resolution. My practice of taking risks had amazing results. Not only did I reach my target of donations to the fund, but I had many more positive and engaging encounters than I'd had in the first five weeks. On one occasion, the risk I took was telling the householder about my 'taking risks practice'! She was delighted by this and it encouraged her to take an interest in the project. I returned each evening energized and inspired as my resolution gathered momentum and took on a life of its own. By the end of the appeal I had proved to myself that I was capable of more – far more – than I thought I was. And this simply wouldn't have happened if I hadn't committed myself to a target that I secretly thought was beyond my reach. A vague 'I'll do the best I can' would not have activated my energies in this way – and I, as well as the underprivileged in India I was collecting for, would have been all the poorer.

Buddhism says the qualities you need to practise ethics can be fully activated only when you commit yourself to a self-transcending ideal. In other words, what inspires you to be ethical needs to go *beyond* the ethical. Otherwise you just won't be able to get motivated enough. Or you'll be motivated up to a point but no further. Sangharakshita talks about meeting people who are leading an ethical life without the inspiration of an unlimited ideal. He says that you can't exactly *fault* their ethics, but that there is something dead about the way they are practising; their practice is not really alive. The reflection on p.94 will help you identify your values and see how they fit into the context of your life.

Reflection: values

You will need three A4-size sheets of paper and a pen.

Draw a big circle on your first sheet of paper and inside write all the main aspects and activities in your life. Try to arrange it so that things you feel the most emotional connection to and/or that you spend the most time doing are nearer the centre. Things that are less important to you *or* that are important to you but you spend less time on will be nearer the edge, or they may be outside altogether. It works best if you do it quickly, so spend up to five minutes doing this.

Now, on the second sheet of paper, brainstorm your values, again writing them down quickly, in about five minutes. Perhaps you value friendship and community, beauty, the opportunity to contribute.

Now draw a big circle on your third sheet of paper and place the elements of your life as they'd be if you were being true to your values. What would ideally be at the centre? What would be nearer the edge? Would anything new come in?

Now look at your first and third sheets of paper together. Are they very different or similar? If they are similar, you could reflect on the conditions you've put in place to achieve that and resolve to maintain them. If they are different, you could resolve to take one concrete step to help move towards your true values in life. For instance, you might decide to sign up for a meditation course, spend half an hour playing with your kids, or take a poetry book with you to read on the Tube instead of reading the free newspapers. You could even write the date on your sheets of paper and then do the reflection again in a few months and see what changes there have been.

Commitment

In order to arouse your deeper energies, you need first to have a clear sense of what your highest values are – perhaps they are freedom or truth or love. Secondly you need to commit yourself to those values. If you remain half-hearted or indecisive, your full potential won't be activated. In fact, to the extent that you don't commit, notions such as freedom, truth, love, or Enlightenment will remain simply 'bright ideas' rather than ideals.

The notion of commitment seems to be becoming less and less

Not About Being Good

popular. In our consumerist culture we're sold choice, and we're told the more choice we have the more our lives will be enhanced. But without commitment you'll only ever stay on the surface of your life. Commitment draws out your deeper resources. It tests you. It shows you that you are more than you thought. It will enrich you and enable you to contribute something of value to the world – whether that's a poem, a classroom on an Indian railway platform, or a selfless act of generosity.

I met a young woman at the Buddhist Centre recently whose attendance at our winter retreat had given her a deeper sense of the possibilities of Buddhist practice. She said that, as a result, she was going to give the teachings and practices her best shot for the rest of the year. At the end of that time she would assess their effect and make an informed choice about whether or not she wanted to carry on. I thought this was a highly intelligent approach. It combines the twin principles of commitment and freedom. You have to be free to make your own choices; free in order to commit. In other words, free not to be a Buddhist in order to be a Buddhist.[2] At the same time, without a degree of commitment, you'll never really know if the practices work. You'll have nothing to base your choice on.

Commitment isn't a once-and-for-all thing. There will always be deepening levels of it, and Triratna Buddhism offers a path to express key points within those deepening levels. I've outlined the process of this path in the section headed 'Commitment in Triratna' on p.102.

Becoming ordained as a Buddhist means making a formal commitment to the ideals of Buddhism. There is nothing abstract about this. It means committing to making those ideals more and more active in every part of your life. As a primary means of doing this, Triratna Order members take the ten precepts. As we saw in Chapter 4, the ten precepts are training principles that are together aimed at relating to actions of body, speech, and, most importantly, mind. This is because someone becoming an Order member is pledging to make her commitment manifest in the transformation of every aspect of her being. More specifically and significantly, she takes the three mind precepts at ordination because she accepts her ordination for the attainment of Enlightenment for the benefit of all beings. This means consciously intending to purify her mind of ignorance – because this is the only way that Enlightenment can be realized.

In the ordination ceremony, the precepts are taken, in the form of vows, from the person's preceptors. This isn't in the sense of something being handed over to her or even handed on to her. It's not that now she has permission to observe the ten precepts. It's more that she sees that her preceptors are actually living those precepts. The Buddha's teaching is a living tradition, an active force, and, by accepting the precepts, she is continuing that living tradition of ethical behaviour. You could say that the new Order member sees her preceptors becoming more and more truly human, and that sparks off a deeper humanity in her.

When I became ordained, not only did I become more aware of the impact my behaviour had on myself and on particular individuals. I also became more aware that my behaviour impacted on the whole Buddhist community. At ordination I committed my life to helping to build a community working together for the benefit of all beings. But working with others is difficult! They do things in different ways, see things in different ways, even see the spiritual life in different ways. I remember clearly my first big falling out with someone. Convinced he was in the wrong, I was all set to do what I'd always done in my life – to simply dismiss him, have nothing to do with him anymore. But then I realized – somewhat to my dismay I must confess – that to do so would be to make a complete mockery of any notion I had of creating community. To live up to my values – the ideals that I had committed to – I was going to have to find a genuine way of resolving the difficulty. I was going to have to call on deeper inner reserves. As on the fundraising appeal, I found that I was capable of more than I thought and I was able to get back into harmony. Without calling on my commitment, or perhaps I should say without my commitment calling on me, those deeper inner reserves that enabled me to find a genuinely creative way forward would have simply remained untapped. I would have believed I had done the best I could and that asking more of myself was impossible and unreasonable.

Of course not everyone will want to become ordained. But the principle of commitment still holds true. Whatever your values are, your level of commitment to them will affect the way your behaviour unfolds. It will affect whether or not they become truly lived ideals or remain notional wishes or pious hopes. Your level of commitment

Not About Being Good

will give you something to live up to and the incentive to live up to it. And the more limitless your ideal, the less your energy will be thwarted by obstacles in the pursuit of living up to it; the more fully you'll be able to give yourself wholeheartedly.

Practical action

In practical terms, committing to the precepts means resolving to do everything you can to keep them. It means resolving to return continually to them: to be alert to any breaches of them, to face the fact of any breaches, and to get 'back on track' straight away (I'll be looking in detail at how to do this in Chapter 6). Committing to the precepts means, at the very least, not wilfully maintaining a state of a stubborn or grim unforgiving attitude where you don't even want to hear the other person say they're sorry, because then you'd have to moderate your own states of mind. It means not actively harbouring unskilful states of mind like that fictional Scottish lady, Tam O'Shanter's wife Kate, awaiting her husband's return home from his drinking session,

> *Gathering her brows like a gathering storm*
> *Nursing her wrath to keep it warm.*[3]

Committing to the precepts also means cultivating mindfulness so that you don't let yourself get to 'breaking point' where you think, 'That's it; I've had enough of trying to be skilful.' A friend of mine calls this pressing the 'sod-off' button. Mindfulness will help you to see those moments coming and pre-empt them.

And, finally, committing to the precepts means resolving to put yourself in conditions that will support you to keep them. It's worth considering this, as often we don't realize just how much conditions influence us.

I've never forgotten a radio interview I heard given by an old British soldier from the Second World War. He told how during the war he'd come across the body of a dead German soldier, and saw he was carrying a watch-case. He described how he said to himself, 'That's a good-looking watch – I'll have that', and unpinned the case from the dead man's uniform. When he opened it, however, he saw that inside, instead of the watch he'd expected, was a photo of the dead man's wife and child. The sight of this affected him deeply. He said he suddenly realized that in other circumstances that man could have been 'the best friend of my life'. And he put the watch-case carefully back. On the radio interview he started weeping as he described how, at that moment, he'd appreciated just how much the war had coarsened his own sensibilities. He said he'd suddenly come to his senses and realized, 'I'm not the sort of person who takes another man's watch.' He was weeping violently now over the airwaves, saying, 'That's what war does to you. That's what war does.'

Most of us, most of the time, will mirror the situations we find ourselves in. We're far less individual and far more easily influenced than we think. The situations we find or put ourselves in will tend to either coarsen or refine our ethical sensibilities. So for a very long time in our spiritual journeys, setting up the conditions to support ourselves living up to our values is actually the main work. It's the most constructive area to put our energy. This is why at the Buddhist Centre we encourage people to go on retreat. On a retreat we try to create the best possible conditions to support skilful behaviour through reducing input, regular meditation, explicitly exploring deeper human values, and creating community. Of course you can't be on retreat all the time but your experience on retreat will remind you what your true values actually are. It will reinforce those values.

Tragically for the old soldier, his was a condition that couldn't easily have been changed, and sometimes that will be the case for us. But very often we can influence our conditions. And committing to ethical practice means taking responsibility for actually doing that. If you're serious about practising the precepts, it's intelligent to think of what conditions you need to put into place to keep to your intentions. The Buddhist word for the quality you need in order to be on the alert for situations and events that are likely to lead you away from your intentions and into unskilful action is appamāda. This is usually translated as 'mindfulness', as when we say the final words of the Buddha were, 'With mindfulness, strive on.'[4] But 'appamāda' means 'mindfulness' in the particular sense of keeping up mindful attention in order to guard against

Not About Being Good

being taken unawares and led into unskilfulness. A more precise translation is 'non-heedlessness'.[5]

Practising appamāda means having the intelligence to ask yourself, 'What obstacles to skilful behaviour might I encounter, and what strategies might I employ? How am I going to remind myself to do this?' It means letting go of any pride that makes you want to do everything 'under your own steam', without supportive conditions.

For example, if you know you always fall back into old negative patterns when you go to spend a long weekend with your family, you could take a picture of the Buddha to remind yourself of your values. Or you could arrange in advance to phone a friend halfway through – one whom you know will genuinely help you and not collude. Or if you've decided not to drink alcohol during the week, maybe you need to have a chat with your partner ahead of time, telling them why you're doing it and asking for their support. Or if you're trying to be vegetarian but about to travel abroad where it will be harder to get vegetarian food, maybe you can look up some websites beforehand so that you can go prepared. If you practice heedfulness in these ways, you'll be supporting yourself to live up to your true values instead of allowing yourself to take the path of least resistance whenever the going gets tough, and thus undermining your commitment.

Lifeblood

The relationship between commitment and actual practice of the Buddhist path is a dynamic one, a living one. Sangharakshita talks of the commitment to the ideals of Buddhism as 'one's lifeblood as a Buddhist' and the observance of the precepts as 'the circulation of that blood through every fibre of one's being'. And blood has to circulate. If it isn't circulating, the organism to which it belongs is, by definition, dead.[6]

If the young woman I spoke to after the winter retreat does indeed spend a whole year actually practising ethics, meditation, and reflection, as she goes along she'll understand herself and the nature of what she has committed to in newer and more subtle ways – ways she could never have previously imagined.

I started this chapter by saying that the ideal of Enlightenment is what underpins a Buddhist ethical life. But in fact none of us really knows what Enlightenment is. We can't know. The only way we will know is by becoming Enlightened ourselves. Given that, depending on the ideal of Enlightenment to give value and meaning to our ethical practice may seem paradoxical. In fact it's a paradox that's natural to any creative process. For example, it was only by committing myself to writing this book and actually making my best attempt to write it that I began to gain the understanding and appreciation of what 'writing a book' might actually mean. From this perspective I could see that I simply had no idea what 'writing a book' meant before starting out – even though I committed myself to doing it. The more seriously I applied myself to it, the more it demanded from me. The realms of what *could* be possible in 'writing a book' and how much I had to learn to even approach those realms became more apparent. It certainly made me appreciate other authors who have gone before me in a completely new way. In other words I appreciated the goal – and my distance from it – more fully, which in turn drew me on.

A poem by Seamus Heaney has the lines,

> *The art of oil painting –*
> *Daubs fixed on canvas – is a paltry thing*
> *Compared with what cries out to be expressed*[7]

These lines seem to convey the anguish you may sometimes feel as you realize the inadequacy of your efforts in the light of the ideals you're trying to express. Sometimes it can even feel as if you've taken several steps backwards and that you're less skilful now than when you started out. As you commit yourself more deeply, your most familiar unskilful impulses can seem to manifest with greater strength than ever, which can be alarming and even result in you feeling thoroughly ashamed and inadequate. I've seen Buddhists (including myself) who've been practising for twenty or thirty years destabilized by the forces of doubt, lust, terror, or jealousy that have assailed them. When this happens, I find it helpful to reflect on the story of the Buddha and the attack of Mara.

The story is set on the night of the Buddha's Enlightenment. The Buddha sat down to meditate with the words,

Not About Being Good

Gladly would I let the flesh and blood in my body dry up, leaving just the skin, tendons, and bones, but if I have not attained what can be reached through human firmness, human persistence, human striving, there will be no relaxing my persistence.[8]

He was totally committed. Suddenly he was assailed by the armies of Mara. Mara represents all the forces that hold us back, and in the legend he's personified as ferociously powerful. First of all Mara sent his sons to attack the Buddha with fierce weapons. But as the hurled weapons reached the aura of the Buddha they were transformed to flowers, which fell gently at the Buddha's feet. Then Mara sent his beautiful daughters to try to seduce the Buddha. The Buddha remained unperturbed. Finally Mara tried his last trick. He came close to the Buddha and whispered, 'What right have you to sit here thinking you can attain Enlightenment? Who do you think you are?' The Buddha simply reached down and touched the earth with his right fingertips. At that the spirit of the earth, the earth goddess, rose up and bore witness to all the Buddha's skilful actions throughout lifetimes and Mara, completely defeated, slunk away.

This story says to me that it's usually at times when you're about to take a significant spiritual step forward that 'Mara' – representing all the forces within us that hold us back, all the work still to be done – will appear. And it can really feel as though you're being assailed by something not in your control. How you respond when this happens is the vital thing. If you act out of these impulses – proposition your friend's wife, lose your temper with your colleague, or allow doubt to dissuade you – then that will have negative karmic consequences for you. It will undermine you, as well as causing harm in the world. But if you can do as the Buddha did, sit steady, take confidence from all the skilful efforts you've been making, and let the forces burn themselves out, you'll have turned what seemed painful and even felt like a step back into a gift. You'll have transformed yourself at a level of consciousness that hitherto was unavailable to you. You'll have become integrated at a much deeper level.

In Chapter 1 we explored the path of integration and ways to work at becoming more integrated. Committing to a self-transcending ideal is the most potent way of all of becoming integrated. In committing to any ideal, first of all your positive energies will be aroused – as my determination was aroused during the fundraising appeal. Then your negative energies will be converted – as my fear was converted during that appeal. Then, the more self-transcending your ideal is, the more your unconscious energies will be brought into the light of day, giving you the opportunity to transform them. In other words the ideal will draw all the disparate parts of you together – even parts of you you've been unaware of. All these parts of you will become focused and start moving in a more skilful direction, that is, in the direction of the ideal. Chase Twichell expresses this beautifully in a poem about going to meet a Buddhist teacher. Here the teacher is the personification of the ideal. The poem ends:

> *I heard*
> *his bare feet on the wood floor.*
>
> *All the slow fish of ignorance*
> *turned towards that sound.*[9]

Commitment in Triratna

In the Triratna Buddhist Community, if someone is becoming serious about Buddhism, then there's the opportunity to become a mitra, which means 'friend'. A mitra of the Triratna Buddhist Community is someone who, first, feels themselves to be a follower of the Buddha; secondly, is practising the five precepts; and thirdly, wants to deepen their exploration of Buddhism within the context of Triratna. The outward expression of these 'three declarations' is a public ceremony. So, on becoming a mitra, someone is ritually marking the fact that she is aligning herself with the ideals of Buddhism and, as an expression of that, trying to live by the five precepts more and more fully. For each person this will express itself differently, but there will also be commonality – for example most mitras would be moving towards being vegetarian (if they weren't fully vegetarian already), as an expression of their practice of the first precept.

If, after they've become a mitra, someone decides she wants to commit herself to the self-transcending ideals such as the ones I've discussed in this chapter, she embarks on a training that leads up

Practice suggestion: cultivating ethical vigilance

Take five or ten minutes to think of the week ahead. Choose one event that you anticipate will be particularly challenging in terms of your being able to stay aware and positive enough to act from the principles expressed in the precepts.

Ask yourself in the here and now: when this event comes around, are you just going to 'let yourself go' or would you like to cultivate appamāda, ethical vigilance?

If the latter, then think of three things you could put in place that would support you when this challenging event comes around. Write them down now.

After the event has happened, make the time to reflect again. Did your efforts to cultivate appamāda help? What did you learn? Write down some reflections.

Fig. 4: The Three Jewels

to her ordination ceremony. While becoming a mitra represented experiencing the beginnings of a Buddhist perspective on life, now she is aspiring to deepen her commitment to the Buddhist ideals to the point where that commitment is active in all aspects of her life and has enough momentum to be sustained for the duration of her life.

As part of symbolizing their commitment, at ordination every new Order member in Triratna is given a kesa to wear around his or her neck. The kesa was originally a belt – traditionally, when you became ordained as a monk, robes were given to you and the belt hung around your neck, so the kesa derives from that. If you go to a Triratna centre you'll see Order members wearing them. The emblem on the kesa depicts the Three Jewels of Buddhism (see Figure 4). The yellow jewel is the Buddha or the ideal of Enlightenment; the blue jewel is the Dharma, the teachings of the Buddha; the red jewel is the Sangha, the spiritual community. The Three Jewels are surrounded by flames, representing spiritual transformation, and they're resting upon a red lotus flower, representing the practice of the precepts. Each new Order member is also given a Pali or Sanskrit name. All of these names convey spiritual qualities and, most importantly, they signify a spiritual rebirth – an entry into a life that goes beyond the personal.

Chapter six

....

Learning to die

In Chapter 5 we saw that connecting with and committing to the ideals of Buddhism is what sustains practising Buddhist ethics. This chapter is concerned with the fact that, the more you connect with value and commit to value, the more acting in ways that go against it will feel painful. You'll feel the pain of letting yourself down, of hurting others, of not living up to your ideals. And the more you have committed to living a life of value, and the higher those values are, the more acute this pain will be.

Remorse not guilt

The Buddhist word for this painful awareness is hrī, which means remorse. The most important thing to remember about hrī is that, although it's painful, it's positive. It's painful because you've gone against the values that you've set your heart upon. It's positive because you only experience it to the extent that you have values in the first place and the sensitivity to notice you've gone against them.

This means that people usually feel more hrī the longer and the more intensively they practise Buddhist ethics, because their ethical sensitivity increases and their standards are raised. For example, I used to think it was fine to 'speak my mind' – which in effect meant speaking harshly – if I was angry with someone. It would cause me no remorse or hrī whatsoever. In fact I was rather proud of what I thought of as my 'fiery temperament', and thought others should just 'deal with it'. These days I still haven't completely overcome the tendency to let my anger and irritation spill out. But, through practising and reflecting on the precepts, I'm much more acutely aware of the harm my harsh speech causes to others, and much more aware of the possibility of acting differently. Those things combine to mean that hrī arises more readily. This painful regret, in turn, becomes an incentive to act more skilfully in the future.

I'll be spending a good bit of this chapter outlining a series of steps you can take when you notice the arising of hrī. But first there's an important distinction to make, one that I could even say changed my life when I found out about it: the distinction is that this hrī or remorse is not the same thing as guilt.

Before I was a Buddhist I used to think guilt was a virtue. In fact the worse I felt about myself for various things I'd done, the more virtuous I thought I was. Looking back I see now that what I was doing was a sort of protection, even a cop-out: if I felt bad enough about myself it would prove I was really sorry and, most importantly, no one would have the heart to get angry with me or punish me. As Oscar Wilde puts it,

> There is a luxury in self-reproach. When we blame ourselves, we feel that no one else has a right to blame us.[1]

So, as you can imagine, it was a bit of a shock to me to find out that guilt itself would be classed as an unskilful mental state in Buddhism. One of the reasons for this is that, paradoxically, going round in this state of guilt, horrible as it might feel, is not actually facing up to your own ethical behaviour. It's a perverse, convoluted, and unpleasant way of avoiding it, and I speak from experience!

In distinguishing guilt from remorse or hrī, I find Sangharakshita's identification of three things that happen in (usually quick) succession to produce guilt[2] really invaluable.

He says that first there is the consciousness that you have done something wrong – or at least done something that someone else did not want you to do.

Secondly, there is the fear of being punished when you are found out, or, if you haven't actually done anything yet, the fear of punishment if you were to do it and get caught. Of course this leads to complications like secrecy and concealment and a general feeling of resentment. But the third factor is probably the most telling one of all. The person who does not want you to do the thing may be someone you love and who loves you – in other words someone on whom you are emotionally dependent. If you do what they don't

Not About Being Good

want you to do, they will not only punish you, they will withdraw their love from you.

It may be an actual person, or an internalized 'authority figure', or an assembly of people including both actual people and internalized authorities. It's hard to live with the disapproval or the implied disapproval of those around us: our family, people at work, society in general. In my own case I slowly began to realize that my feeling guilty, my punishing myself, in effect, was a desperate way of trying to avoid the scenario where I'd be punished by the withdrawal by others of love, acceptance, and approval.

There's an old joke about a man who goes to confession in a Catholic church and confesses he stole some chickens. Before the priest gives him his absolution he asks, 'How many chickens was it?' 'Two, Father,' says the man, 'but make it three and I'll get another on the way back!' I know that this is an oversimplified caricature of Catholic confession, but the point is that, if you get caught in the cycle of doing-what-you-think-you-shouldn't/guilt/doing-what-you-think-you-shouldn't/guilt, you'll hardly know what comes first anymore. You can end up going round in a perpetual state of guilt, and seeing a list of precepts will only add to your horror. You'll easily see the precepts as just more oppressions, just more things to feel guilty about. You'll try to counter that, perhaps talking about 'not beating yourself up' or 'not giving yourself a hard time'. But this will not get to the roots of guilt in a deep enough way to transform it. The only way to do that is to try to understand it more deeply.

The notion of guilt depends on the notion of sin. And the notion of sin depends on some outside authority. Sin essentially works on the basis of obedience rather than consent.[3] As we've seen, there is no external authority in Buddhism – this means there can be no notion of sin either. As Sangharakshita has memorably stated,

> belief in sin is nothing but a stumbling block that arises out of
> treating rules as ends in themselves.[4]

It's a stumbling block because we waste time worrying about how to get rid of it. And it's a real danger because, as we've seen, the tendency to treat rules as ends in themselves and to allow the Buddhist notions of 'skilful' and 'unskilful' to degenerate into the absolutes of 'good' and 'bad' – in other words to succumb to literalism – is very strong. So, even though most of us these days don't believe that there is somewhere called 'hell' where we will eternally suffer after we die for things we've done on earth while we're alive, we're not necessarily immune from the tendency to veer towards thinking in absolutes. I've come to think that it's not so much that theological religious conditioning has resulted in our general tendency to literal-mindedness, but rather that it is our tendency, as human beings, to literal-mindedness that has produced theologies. Then, when the theologies become untenable or seem absurd, we get rid of them. But, if we haven't addressed the tendency to literal-mindedness, it will creep back in. We'll end up treating the Buddhist precepts, at least in their negative formulation, as a set of things that are 'wrong in themselves'. It's easy to fool ourselves that we are above such literal-mindedness but, if we had gone beyond it, we would never ever take the moral high ground with regard to someone else's unskilfulness. Rather, seeing that their actions would, under the law of karma, be bound up with suffering for them, we'd feel love and compassion.

If you want to become more ethically skilful, it's crucial that you learn to tell the difference between guilt and remorse because guilt is paralyzing. This is another reason that it's regarded in Buddhism as a negative mental state. It stops you from moving towards any self-transcending ideals. Remorse, on the other hand, is the opposite. It's the first step in moving from unskilfulness to skilfulness, and therefore towards value. But it's not always easy to tell the difference, and they're often mixed up together.

If in doubt, one question you can ask yourself is, 'Have I actually broken a precept?' Guilt tends to befuddle the mind so you can use the list of precepts to bring clarity into your mind. If the answer to your question is 'no', then you have probably succumbed to guilt. For example, I can be plagued with unease due to the fact I can never seem to get to the bottom of my e-mail inbox. In fact, I often start e-mails with, 'I'm sorry it's taken me so long to respond.' But have I actually broken any precepts? If, on reflection, I can see that I haven't gone against any of the ethical precepts, then I know that what I am feeling cannot be hrī. I know I've succumbed to guilt, a sort of vague but pernicious feeling that 'people' will think I'm not very good at my job and so they won't like me.

By contrast, just because you feel guilty doesn't mean you haven't been unskilful! Guilt and hrī can get mixed up. One rule of thumb I've remembered for years – someone came up with it in a study group I was in – is 'Guilt is a concern with yourself; remorse is a concern with the other person (that is, the person you've been unskilful in relation to).' Guilt is not really facing what you've done, whereas remorse is facing that squarely. You can see it quite pragmatically. If you've broken a precept, you've put an obstacle in the way of your spiritual development. What you need to do is get back on the right path. Sin doesn't come into it.

So hrī is natural because it doesn't depend on the approval or disapproval of any outside agent or authority. It does, however, depend on your own ethical sensibility being quite developed. A close neighbour of hrī is apatrāpya, which means something like 'respect for wise opinion'. This is quite hard to define. It could easily sound as if it meant fear of the disapproval of others, which it isn't at all. It's more that in the company of some people – especially people you genuinely look up to and are inspired by – you just don't want to be unskilful. This is not because you fear such people will disapprove of you, but because their very being seems to communicate, 'This is what it's like to be more fully human; this is what's possible.' You suddenly find you don't want to be mean or petty any more when you're with them; they bring out the best in you. This is not because of anything they say, but because of who they are. And if you do say or do something unskilful in their presence, they don't collude with you. They certainly won't punish you, but they don't try to protect you from the consequences of your actions either. In this way, they are like an externalized conscience for you. Because often our own sense of conscience is not that developed, it's very helpful to have people in our lives whose opinion we respect enough for apatrāpya to arise.

If you do feel hrī, true remorse, you'll naturally want to make amends – where possible. I once knew someone who travelled round Ireland replacing everything he'd ever stolen: a tin opener from a B&B here, a towel from a guest house there. This example may seem a little dramatic – but I wanted to include it to show that making amends may mean going to some trouble and that there's value in taking that trouble.

As well as making amends, if you feel hrī you'll want to resolve not to do that thing again. It can be helpful to reflect, maybe with the help of friends, 'What would I do another time in a similar situation? Where did I lose the initiative? What were the conditions that made me lose appamāda (heedfulness)?' You might even realize that there are some situations where you're just not yet able to be skilful. Sometimes certain circumstances will be too much for you – for now. There may be someone you get triggered into negativity by so much that you have to admit to yourself that it would be better to 'cross the road' for the moment rather than getting into discussion with them. Although, of course, to practise Buddhist ethics fully you would want to work towards amending that situation in time. You've got to be intelligent about it. This is part of being skilful.

And it may be appropriate to apologize to someone if you've hurt them. Here I'm not talking about the automatic apology to every lamp post you walk into, the 'pardon-me-for-existing' that can seem to be a common syndrome, a semi-conscious habit.[5] I'm meaning a conscious expression of regret. I'd suggest that, if you do apologize, you make it unqualified – even if you feel you were provoked. What the other person did is their business. It's tempting (again I know from experience) to slip in a justification, even a criticism: 'I'm sorry I yelled, but you were really winding me up.' Even 'I apologize for my part in our argument' is a kind of implied criticism. (My hackles always rise when someone says that to me.) Even 'I'm sorry I yelled, but I was trying to show how strongly I felt' has a diluting effect. Try practising just, 'I'm sorry I yelled.' It will probably make you feel more exposed, more naked. But that's not a bad thing. Apology is a spiritual act because it is a deliberate letting go of self.

Confession

As a Catholic child, I was an avid confession-goer. When we were six, our teacher, Mrs Grimley, explained that each of us had a soul that was white like a white handkerchief. Every time we committed a sin, it was as if a blot of ink stained the handkerchief. When we died the state of our souls would be inspected by God, and this would determine the length of our stay in purgatory (unless, of course, we had a mortal sin – such as murder or missing Sunday mass – completely blackening our soul, in which case we would burn in hell for eternity). She told us that the fires of purgatory burnt just as fiercely as the fires of hell, the only difference was that purgatory would come, eventually, to an end. Every week I went to confession, imagining my soul stained with my sins. So desperate was I to have my soul returned to its pure-white-handkerchief state that I'd sit beside the confessional on my own, like a dog sitting outside its kennel, until the priest, probably with a sigh, admitted me. Then I could tell him about being cheeky to my mother, not doing what my father told me, calling my little sisters names, and receive my penance of a decade of the rosary. But things went seriously wrong when, at the fairground, I put a ha'penny into the Penny Falls slot instead of a penny. I already knew, from a previous stern warning from the priest when I'd cheated at a game of Monopoly, that to cheat with money was particularly bad. So I was too frightened to admit this sin committed in the fairground. But omitting it from my confession meant I'd added the sin of lying to the sin of cheating. It could only get worse. The next week I added another lie to the sin, and a lie to the lie. And so on – my sins heaping up exponentially. At some point I gave up going to confession altogether. Looking back I see that even at my most sincere and devout, I never had any conception that going to confession could actually change me. Try as I might I would repeat the same sins week after week. The Penny Falls incident had put paid to my best hope: that I would drop down dead immediately after I'd received absolution, my soul pristine.

Now, once again, as a Buddhist, I regularly take part in the practice of confession. But this time round it's without the idea of an external force to appease, without the notion of the stain of sin, without the notion even of a soul to be stained. Sometimes I confess with one other person; a good friend I know will take me seriously, someone who shares my values and will understand my purpose. That's all you need to start a confession practice. Other times I confess within a small group of people who are also committed to the ideals of Buddhism, and whom I meet with regularly.

Practice suggestion: setting up a confession practice

Who to confess to. It's important to confess to someone who will take you seriously; someone who will understand what it is you are doing; someone who shares your values; someone who can maybe help you with working out how to avoid the unskilful action next time, or who can gently point out that you've been confessing the same thing for some time now and you may need a clearer strategy to avoid that particular unskilfulness. You could confess with one other person or as part of a group.

A word of caution. Do take care not to knock someone off balance by confessing something that involves them when they didn't know anything about it. It can be quite difficult to be on the receiving end of someone, especially in a group situation, confessing their resentment, jealousy, or whatever of you. As a friend of mine once said, 'Just because you're practising confession doesn't mean you can ignore the speech precepts!' So be timely, harmonizing, helpful, and sensitive in your confessions as well as truthful. You can still confide or confess those emotions, but do it with someone else first, and perhaps talk over with them whether it would be a good idea to tell the person affected. And choose someone to confide in who doesn't also feel any kind of unskilfulness with regard to that person. Otherwise it's all too easy for the communication to degenerate into collusion, into 'ganging up'. It's better to pick someone who actually likes that person. Your willingness or unwillingness to do that in itself is a clue to how much you really want to change.

When to confess. It's best to confess as soon as possible, while you still feel that spark of hrī, before you talk yourself out of it. It can be helpful to have a regular slot for confession, say once a week. This is because (as with most things that involve us changing) there's bound to be a natural resistance and making it a regular positive habit can help to overcome this.

How to confess. It's helpful to mark the beginning and end of a confession period. And some people like to receive confessions formally by a phrase such as, 'I hear and accept your confession, may you be purified', and save any questions or discussion until after that ritual acceptance. It can also be helpful to name the precept or precepts you've broken. This helps to make things even more conscious. There's no hard and fast rule about all this. Probably the only 'rule' is to spend some time together deciding the format before you start.

What to confess. The simplest is to confess all the actions that have gone against your ideals. The more you can be specific about your actual behaviour, the better. It may make you sound very spiritual to 'confess' that you haven't thought about Enlightenment all week, but it's more effective, and takes more courage actually, to confess to the mean streak that made you join in the office gossip about a colleague. I always remember one person who had a weekly confession practice within a particular group telling me about his practice. He said the group would all sit there quietly first and he'd be thinking, 'Oh yes I can confess this and that and such-and-such', but then something would creep into his awareness, with the simultaneous thought, 'Oh no, no, I could never confess *that!*' *That* of course was the real confession that he had to make.

Many people also find it helpful to supplement their confession practice with a practice of disclosing long-term tendencies and deep-seated habits such as fault-finding, anxiety, guilt, or comparison. Although you may not be able to let go of and confess these all at once, bringing them into consciousness can be a significant step in transforming them.

I confess because, even though when I've been unskilful I try to apologize, make amends, and recognize the conditions that led to me being unskilful in the first place, I need something else, something even more potent to help me to transform the basic tendencies of mind that govern my actions.

The practice of confession is a ritualized way of fully acknowledging that you have been unskilful and that you intend to move on. The unskilfulness may have been in relation to someone else, or it may be that you have been harsh or unkind towards yourself, perhaps through critical internal narratives, or perhaps through punishing behaviour such as self-harm. By actually articulating what you've done and your intention not to repeat that unskilful behaviour to another person, or a group of people, you bring your actions and their underlying intentions into fuller consciousness. I find that the immediate effect of this is to intensify any feelings of remorse or hrī – it's important to remember that it is highly positive. Practising confession in the Buddhist sense, without guilt, will have an ongoing effect too. It will render your conscience more tender. It will actually modify the quality of your consciousness and make you more ethically aware. Confession also helps deepen friendship and build a sense of spiritual community. People sometimes say that you need trust to confess. This is true, of course, but at the same time the practice of confession also builds trust.

If you'd like to set up a practice of confession, I've drawn up a practical guide in the box on pages 112–13. It isn't exhaustive and I'm sure you'll add things to it along the way, but these are things I've found useful over the years.

What you do after you've made a confession is really important. The reason any of us are unskilful in the first place is that we, to some extent, at least in that moment, have lost touch with our values. So the thing to pay urgent attention to is to get back in touch with your values and your motivation in regard to them. This is why guilt is so bad for you: by tying you in its knot, it prevents you having any sort of perspective and so it actively prevents you getting back in touch with your values. There are a number of ways to get back in touch. You could read something that inspires you. You could bring to mind people who inspire you. You could remind yourself of your motivation to help bring more positivity into the suffering world. Some people like to end their confession practice by rejoicing in something positive they've done. You could reflect that confession itself is a very positive action. I remember I'd confessed something quite weighty in the journal for personal communication that we have in our Order. A few days later I had a postcard from Bali from an Order member I hardly knew saying, 'As I'm writing this there is a woman in a beautiful silk sari walking past. But your confession is even more beautiful than that silk sari.' You could reflect that progress is possible for all human beings – including yourself. The reflection opposite will take you through some of the stages of confession.

Someone in a Buddhism class recently asked whether there was any value in penance. I think you have to be quite careful here. If you used the notion of penance intelligently in order to bring more discipline into your life or to reinspire yourself, then that could be positive. I imagine that was the original meaning of being given a decade of the rosary (a set of ten prayers) or some other prayers as a penance in

Reflection: acknowledgement of regret

Sit quietly, close your eyes, and spend a minute reflecting on each of the five precepts by asking yourself: in the last twenty-four hours, have I had any regrets involving:

- harming a living being;
- taking the not given;
- causing harm within the arena of sex;
- speaking falsely;
- taking intoxicants?

If you have no regrets, that means you are experiencing the positive state of mind of being free from remorse, so you could continue sitting quietly for five minutes enjoying that and letting it naturally deepen.

If you do have regrets, that means you are experiencing the positive state of mind of hrī. If you'd like to, you could write down those regrets, consider if there is a way to make amends, and then ritually dispose of the regrets by burning the paper (if possible), or tearing it into small pieces.

Then, in either case, find a way to connect or reconnect with your inspiration. A simple way to do that is to repeat these lines:

The Buddha was born as we are born;
What the Buddha overcame, we too can overcome;
What the Buddha attained, we too can attain.[6]

Catholic confession. But if penance descends into punishment, a sort of aversion therapy, it's doubtful whether it has any spiritual value. If you simply try to bully yourself into being skilful, your consciousness won't be genuinely modified. It won't actually result in your becoming more skilful in the real sense of the word, that is it won't help you in developing the subtle art of cultivating appropriate inner intentions.[7] You'll be in danger of simply getting caught up in a sort of spiritual calorie-counting – a cycle where it doesn't matter which comes first: I went to the gym yesterday so I'm allowed to have pizza today; I've meditated every day for a week so I'm allowed to get drunk tonight.

That isn't to say that you might not have a healthy fear of the consequences of your actions. I remember once sitting in meditation with my usual irritable thoughts gathering momentum in my mind. I suddenly asked myself, 'What will the consequences be of letting these irritable thoughts feed on each other and gather momentum for the rest of my life?' I had an instantaneous vision of myself as a wizened, bad-tempered old lady with no friends. It was horrifying enough to shock me out of the irritable cycle – at least for that meditation anyway. I saw that this in all likelihood would be the natural consequence. It's not that anyone would be meting out punishment. There's no cosmic judge, or need of one. And by the same token, no one, not even a Buddha, can absolve you of the effects of your actions. If you've spent a lot of time being bad-tempered and critical, people will be a bit nervous of you. And even if you completely reform, it will take time for them to 'catch up'. They won't completely trust you all at once. This is your karma playing itself out. There's a moving little corollary to the story of Angulimala, the finger-necklace murderer we met in Chapter 3. Even after Angulimala had become the Buddha's disciple, the villagers still threw stones at him. The Buddha's response was, 'Bear it brother, bear it.' In other words, if Angulimala learnt not to react unskilfully to this further provocation, eventually the negative consequences of his murderous actions would play themselves out. The fact that he was now a disciple of the Buddha, open to the positive influence of the Buddha, you could even say open to the grace of the Buddha, meant he could see those painful consequences in perspective and therefore bear them more easily.

So far I've been talking about hrī that arises for actions that you're doing in the present, as it were. But sometimes, as you become more ethically sensitive, you can feel a strong sense of remorse for things from the past. This can be very powerful at times and can even seem to contradict the Buddhist teachings, which have been suggesting that, the more you practise ethics and awareness, the more 'happiness will follow'. My friend Canute, whom we met in the Introduction and Chapter 1, gave up the world of nightclubs, drinking, and fighting. But, as he meditated and practised ethics, he began to be deeply troubled by regrets at night when he was supposed to be sleeping. When he did sleep he'd have terrible dreams. Another young man came to me quite distressed on one retreat. He'd been practising a meditation where you bring to mind various people and cultivate goodwill towards them.[8] He was distressed because, whoever he brought to mind, all he could think of was the ways in which he'd hurt that person.

Experiences of remorse for past actions will be painful, so it's important to remember that they are positive. As your state of mind becomes clearer and brighter (this can happen particularly on retreat), unskilful things from the past show up in sharper relief. Or, to look at it another way, it's as if you've created a reservoir of positivity large enough, and deep enough, to be able to face past unskilfulness without becoming totally overwhelmed by it. If you have such experiences and you wish to confess them, again that will be helpful in letting them go and moving on. Just take care in choosing your time and place and person, making sure the person or people you are going to confess to are willing, and in the right space to hear. That said, it can be an enormous relief to confess these things, like shedding a load so you become lighter and freer.

Forgiveness

Apology and confession are positively humbling practices. They involve 'stepping down' from your idea of yourself, and usually there's an inner battle involved. You die to what you are so you are free to become what you really can be. This is what Buddhism calls the practice of 'spiritual death'.

Closely connected with apology and confession is the practice of forgiveness. This also is a 'spiritual-death' practice because you have to let go of your fixed position in regard to events.

I remember watching a TV programme as a teenager. It was a set of interviews with families for whom terrible things had happened: a daughter raped and murdered; a son killed by a hit-and-run driver. Half of the families had forgiven and half hadn't. The ones who hadn't were asking, 'Why should they forgive?' They held the stance that there was absolutely no reason to forgive; on the contrary, they had every justification in the world to hold on to their resentment. And I could see their point. From the point of view of 'fairness', forgiveness is outrageous. But then I looked at the families who had forgiven. Although they undoubtedly had pain and sadness etched into their faces, they seemed to be standing more upright, seemed to occupy more space, seemed like people you could connect with if you met them. In contrast, those who hadn't forgiven seemed wizened, smaller, embittered against the world and everyone in it. You could feel for them but you couldn't imagine connecting with them. Those images made a strong impression on me and convinced me of the power of forgiveness.

Still, it's not easy. Recently I ran a seminar on 'Forgiveness and apology' at the Buddhist Centre. I asked, 'Why forgive?' Some people said that holding on to resentment is painful and consumes a huge amount of energy. Others said that not forgiving creates a psychological world of hostility. One woman quietly said that not forgiving is a source of regret when the person dies. Someone else quoted the saying that seeking revenge is like trying to harm someone by drinking poison yourself. Yet another said that not forgiving keeps us stuck in the past. Finally one man said, 'It's pleasurable not to forgive. It gives you a feeling of superiority. You create the story that you're good and they're bad and to give that up is a terrible thing.' I admired him for his honesty and I thought, 'Here is the nub of it.' When you forgive, you are letting go of the possibility of taking revenge, of 'getting even'. You're giving up part of yourself, part of your identity. This is why when you forgive you're partaking in spiritual death.

But you can't – and shouldn't – force yourself to do it. It's a process. A friend of mine suffered sexual abuse at a young age and recovered the memories of this when she started meditating.[9] At first she felt – even cultivated – anger and blame, telling herself that this was the way to feel empowered again. But gradually it became clear to her that this strategy was only making her feel worse. So she decided to engage in the process of forgiveness. She emphasizes that it was a process, rather than a once-and-for-all action. And she stresses that it wasn't that she felt healed and whole again so then she could let go of the anger and blame. It was the opposite. She realized that the only possibility of healing was through forgiveness. Sometimes people say they will forgive if the other person says they're sorry. But what this means, if you look at it closely, is that you're making your own

Not About Being Good

happiness dependent on someone else's actions. You are potentially backing yourself into a dead end.

My friend reflected on the Buddha's teaching that there is so much grief and suffering felt by all of us – and caused by all of us. None of us escapes. She realized that defining herself as a victim had given her a sense of identity that had previously been absent and that made her feel stronger. But she saw that the danger of this approach is that it can lead to a vicious circle in which, to maintain that sense of identity, the anger and hatred must be kept alive. Even though she still now feels the pain of what happened, she doesn't want to blame anyone. She says that, in her heart of hearts, she knows that holding on to resentment means holding on to her own pain.

Although forgiveness feels like giving something up, in fact it's usually the stronger and more positive person who forgives. Genuine forgiveness (as opposed to just resentfully backing down) is a creative, generative act. It doesn't necessarily mean forgetting (although you don't need to hold on to every little thing), and it may even be appropriate to let someone know the effects of their actions. I remember apologizing to our chairman at the Buddhist Centre for losing my temper in a meeting. He immediately forgave me (in fact I'm sure he already had forgiven me). 'But', he said, 'it does have an effect; your acting like that makes my job more difficult.' I must say I felt about the size of a worm. He had held up a mirror, as it were, to my actions. At the same time I felt no resentment from him, only goodwill and affection. Even if someone has been unskilful, you may let them know the effect of that but it's not your business to mete out punishment, whether that's in the form of righteous indignation, complaining to others about their behaviour, or withdrawing your goodwill.

A Buddha, knowing that someone who had been unskilful would, under the natural law of karma, suffer painful consequences, would feel only compassion. In a similar vein, you can't insist that someone else must forgive you. Everyone needs to make that choice for themselves. And again, if the Buddha encountered someone who was not able to forgive, he would recognize that as painful in itself and feel only compassion in response.

Finally, as well as forgiving others, you can practise forgiving yourself. You can practise forgiving yourself for not being perfect. You can practise forgiving yourself for not living up to your ideals all the time, while at the same time striving to live up to your ideals.[10] If you are to make progress towards your ideals, your concern needs to go beyond your failures. This is the aspect we will be looking at in Chapter 7.

 Practice suggestion: apology

The next time you do something to hurt or offend someone, make them an unreserved apology. Remember to observe the speech precepts – be sensitive and choose your time and place. Then simply say, 'I'm sorry for...' without making any qualifications or excuses, and without expecting any particular response.

Afterwards, take some time to reflect on the experience.

- How did making your apology make you feel about yourself?
- How did it make you feel in relation to the other person?

Chapter seven

....

Being reborn

Reflection: sitting with the Buddha

Sit comfortably, in an upright position with your eyes closed. Connect with a sense of your weight dropping down into the floor and into the cushions or chair.

Now tune in to the natural flow of your breath, just following that with your attention.

Now imagine that you are sitting in the presence of the Buddha, who is also sitting still and meditating. Allow the sense of presence of the Buddha to steady and deepen. You could reflect that the Buddha taught and practised this Mindfulness of Breathing.

Continue to sit, aware of your breath and aware of the presence of the Buddha for five minutes (or longer if you want to).

Then relax your imaginative efforts but sit still for another minute or so to absorb the effects of meditation.

At the end of Chapter 6, we saw that, in order for you to make progress towards your ideals, your concern needs to go beyond your failures. The first step in this is to connect once again with those ideals.

For a Buddhist, to connect – or reconnect – with their inspiration in the deepest sense means to connect with the fact that Enlightenment is a human possibility. It is possible for you and it is represented to you by the Buddha. All the teachings of the Buddha are trying to communicate what the Buddha experienced, what he was. And Buddhism is encouraging us, urging us even, to listen for that presence of the Buddha that flows through the teachings.

So it's important to try to deepen our sense of who the Buddha was, even who the Buddha is, as much as we can. When, at one of our introductory Buddhism courses, I ask people what they know about the historical Buddha, some of them can usually tell me that the Buddha was born in northern India. But actually the key thing I always want to draw from that detail isn't the particular geographical location of his birth. What I want to draw out is that the Buddha was born. The fact that the Buddha was born an ordinary human being has profound implications for us – ordinary human beings. It means we can overcome what the Buddha overcame. It means we can attain what the Buddha attained.

The positive precepts

Because it's beyond our current experience, it's impossible for us to fully imagine what the Buddha did attain. Sometimes people see Enlightenment as what is 'left' after all negative behaviour and views have been abandoned. And of course it's true that an Enlightened being has abandoned all negative behaviour and limiting views. But too literal a reading of this can suggest that Enlightenment was there all the time, just waiting to be discovered – like the ten-pound note I always hope I'll have forgotten about and rediscover in the pocket when I get out my winter coat each November. And the trouble with this way of thinking is that it misses out the essentially creative nature of Enlightenment. Ethical practice gives a direct way of getting a sense of this essentially creative nature, especially if you put more of your attention onto the positive precepts.

Our instinct in thinking about ethics is to think in terms of what we won't do. When we confess, for example, it's usually in relation to something we've done that we undertook not to do. Of course this is important; it's the foundation of ethics and therefore the foundation of all Buddhist practice. But if you think only in those terms, you end up with a rather barren approach.

In the Introduction I said that meditation can lead quite naturally to an examination of the existential situation we all find ourselves within. A young woman who came to one of our classes for the first time recently had a simple but strong experience of this. I'd been leading through a meditation called the Mindfulness of Breathing, where you simply return again and again to the sensations of your body breathing. I was instructing people, every time they found their mind had 'gone away', to come back to those sensations. I noticed that this particular woman looked quite shaken at the end of the meditation, so I was glad that when I asked the class how they'd got on she raised her hand. She said that as she'd practised letting go of the familiar trains of thought fuelled by wanting to have something, or wanting something to stop, she'd suddenly thought, 'Who will I be if I don't go down these familiar tracks? I won't recognize myself anymore.' And, another time, someone else, on hearing that the Buddha didn't experience anger, blurted out, 'Then what did he feel?' It can be hard to imagine being without anger, hatred, and craving. We even talk about these as 'human failings', and maybe even feel we'd miss them and be somehow 'less of a person' if they were gone. I remember some years ago I was really struggling with chronic ill-will. I'd tried everything I could think of to work with it – meditation, confession, reflecting on the negative effect it was having on others – none of these seemed to be enough to shift it. Then one day, I was just standing by my window, and it dawned on me that I had so deeply defined myself by the state of perpetual indignation and annoyance that I didn't know who I'd be without it. I felt that I'd be just a thin wisp of smoke, a wraithlike creature, fleshless and bloodless just drifting through the air – which didn't feel particularly attractive.

So, if we're practising ethics, we need something to attract us. We need to feel that we're moving towards something positive. The eleventh-century Tibetan Buddhist Gampopa compares ethics to a field.[1] A field of course is fertile, seeds can be planted in it, harvests can be reaped from it. Comparing ethics to a field is saying that the practice of ethics is essentially productive, essentially creative. It leads on to so much else. And we can see this clearly when we look at the positive formulations of the precepts. There is no limit to the amount of love or generosity or awareness that you can express. Of course practising the positive precepts takes more skill and imagination than abstaining from unskilfulness. But if you want to understand what Enlightenment is, who the Buddha is, the positive precepts are the ones that really need your attention. You could say the positive precepts are the real precepts. It's by practising them and becoming more skilled in them that you'll meet the Buddha, as you yourself become more Buddha-like. In other words, listening for the presence of the Buddha isn't a passive thing. Your understanding of the Buddha will deepen the more you try to be like the Buddha. In the end it's only by becoming a Buddha that you can know the Buddha, that you can meet the Buddha. But the very attempt of trying to do so will change you, will bring you closer.

Sangharakshita has a lovely analogy for this. The analogy starts with a poet writing a poem. The poem flows from the poet as an expression of his or her inspiration. We come along, not so inspired, and read the poem. And we're lifted up, we become inspired, we become closer to the state of mind of the poet.[2] I remember a particular instance of this in my own life. I was tired after a day's work and I went to a friend's house. 'Lie down on these cushions and relax,' she said, 'I'll cook supper and in the meantime you can listen to this CD.' The CD was Ted Hughes reading his *Tales from Ovid*. Within moments I couldn't remain lying down. The power of the poetry and his voice – a voice that seemed to express that the poet knew the heights and depths of the gods, goddesses, and mortals that inhabited that ancient world – forced me to sit bolt upright. I was transfixed, and I remember cycling home along the canals of Dublin that night with the glorious sensation that the whole world had become a poem. In Sangharakshita's analogy the Buddha is like the poet and his actions are the poem. You may not be Enlightened like the Buddha, but if you act in the way the Buddha did, you'll be 'reading the poem', as it were, and you'll be lifted up closer to the realm of the Buddha. You'll be reborn, you could say, in realms closer and closer to the realm of the Buddha.

This potential for uplift, transformation, and rebirth is expressed in the poem 'New Foal',[3] by Ted Hughes himself. It starts in the manner of an ordinary nature poem. A foal is born.

> Yesterday he was nowhere to be found
> In the skies or under the skies.
> Suddenly he's here.

The poem goes on to describe the foal finding its way to standing up on its legs, connecting with its mother, starting to experience physical sensations. We're told that

Soon he'll be almost a horse.

Up until this point what we're involved in is happening within the natural world, within time, within the world of the senses. But in the next lines the poem moves into a new dimension:

He wants only to be Horse,
Pretending each day more and more Horse
Till he's perfect Horse.

Now 'Horse' is given a capital 'H' and the article 'a' is taken away to show that we're no longer hearing about 'a horse' in time and space, but about archetypal Horse, ideal Horse. And the foal wants only to be Horse. That's the entirety of its longing, that's all it wants. This reminds me of the vision the Buddha had upon his Enlightenment. He saw all humanity like lotuses in a giant pool. Most of them were down in the mud, but here and there some were raised from the mud and some were even fully opened. In this vision the Buddha saw that all human consciousness contains within itself the seeds of its own transcendence. Furthermore, he saw that we will never be fully satisfied until we reach our highest potential. This isn't to say that there is nothing pleasurable or satisfying about life, but that until Enlightenment there will always be that sense of 'there's more I could be' – just as in the poem the foal knows that it has the potential not just to be 'a horse' but to be Horse and it won't be fully satisfied until it has realized that potential.

And the foal moves closer to being Horse by 'Pretending each day more and more Horse'. Obviously sometimes we use the word 'pretend' to mean something like 'play-act', even to mean acting in a way that's hypocritical, but I don't think that's what's meant here. 'Pretend' also means 'to stretch or reach forward, or to direct one's course'.[4] This is what the foal is doing. It directs its course towards being Horse. And the foal does this day by day. It isn't wishful thinking. It's a steady, patient yet persistent effort, in exactly the same way as the practice of the positive precepts is a steady, patient, persistent effort.

And the foal makes this effort, 'Till he's perfect Horse'. The notion of perfection is interesting. We talk about the Buddha as 'the perfection of the human' but this doesn't mean that the Buddha has reached some sort of end point. In fact, for something to be perfect it has to be reaching beyond itself. It has to be constantly transcending. It has to be continually being reborn. This means there's actually no such thing as static perfection. You could even say, paradoxically, that for something to be perfect it has to be imperfect.

Constant creativity

And while you can't really say there's room for improvement in a Buddha, there will always be room for further expression. Enlightenment isn't something you have like a ten-pound note in your pocket, or even a jewel inside you; that's far too static a way of thinking about it. Enlightenment is a way of being. It's essentially responsive. In Chapter 3 we learnt how the historical Buddha met Kisagotami, grieving and in denial over her dead baby, and a particular response was drawn forth from him. But if he'd met someone else instead, in quite a different condition, a different response would have been drawn forth. We know for certain that it would have been a compassionate response, completely purified of self-clinging. But that compassionate response could have taken form in any number of ways.

We have examples in the stories of the Buddha's life, but they are just illustrating the principles. The principles themselves are infinitely applicable. You can be sure that telling her to go and find a mustard seed wasn't the Buddha's stock answer every time in his long life he met a grieving mother. Above all, this story illustrates that the Buddha had more resources available – more imagination, more awareness of Kisagotami, more awareness of what would really help – than everyone else in the situation. This essential quality of responsiveness is the reason why hypothetical debates about imaginary 'ethical dilemma' scenarios aren't really worth the bother, in fact are probably missing the point. Picasso wrote:

> There are painters who transform the sun into a yellow spot, but there are others who, thanks to their art and their intelligence, transform a yellow spot into the sun.[5]

If you look to Buddhism for stock answers and aren't prepared to use your imagination, you'll be turning the sun into 'a yellow spot'.

But if you develop your intelligence and art and skill in practising the precepts, especially the positive ones, you'll transform the yellow spots of your actions into the sun. Or, more prosaically, the best thing you can do is train yourself as intelligently as possible in the precepts, and this will make your mind and heart more agile so you have a better chance of doing what is best at any time, and in any situation.

Enlightenment is a state of constant creativity. It isn't an end point – it's only the furthest point on the horizon of our imagination. And in terms of your own ethical life, Buddhism says it has to be always pointing beyond itself; the total process is always unfinished. Poets are very aware of this. Here's Norman MacCaig, describing a July evening:

> Something has been completed
> That everything is part of,
>   Something that will go on
> Being completed forever[6]

And Tomas Tranströmer, on being human:

> Don't be ashamed to be a human being, be proud!
> Inside you one vault after another opens endlessly.
> You'll never be complete, and that's as it should be.[7]

The positive precepts are infinite in their scope and I like to think that in practising them we are trying to make our lives into works of art, into something beautiful. I often think that in fact it would be much better to think in terms of acting beautifully, or creating beauty, rather than 'being ethical'.

This approach is fundamentally different from the 'tick-list' approach to life, where you go through each day, each week, your whole life, with an attitude of, 'there, that's that done', as you cross off each task. And it shows that, in practising the spiritual life, even Enlightenment itself will express itself differently, will manifest differently, through different people. There's a lovely illustration of this in an early Buddhist text called the Mahāgosiṅga Sutta.[8] The sutta tells of a meeting of six of the Buddha's disciples in a sala-tree forest for a discourse on the full-moon night. One of them, Sariputta, asks each one of the others in turn, 'What kind of monk would illuminate this sala-tree forest?' One says, 'A monk who can pass on the teachings'; another, 'A monk who loves seclusion and meditation'; another, 'A monk with panoramic awareness'; another, 'A monk with few desires'; another says 'Two monks whose discussions are meaningful, harmonious, timely and beneficial'. Then Sariputta himself says, 'A monk who has power over his mind would illuminate the forest.' And finally they ask the Buddha who says:

> The monk who sits in a cross-legged posture, keeping his body straight and mindfulness established and determines, 'until my mind is released without desires, I would not change this posture', illuminates this sala-tree forest.

In this way each disciple, and then the Buddha himself, describes their own particular qualities. Each is different, but all illuminate the forest.

A beautiful life

Emphasizing beauty helps to counteract the tendency that some people (I'm afraid I'm one of them) have of using their idea of the spiritual life as a reason to give themselves, or others, a hard time. Sometimes they do this without really knowing that they are doing it, or why – they just can't seem to stop looking for suffering of some kind. They think anything pleasurable will demand compensation in some way in the manner of the dour 1950s Scottish fish-shop woman in Alastair Reid's poem. Someone greets her with an exclamation of what a beautiful day it was:

> *And what did she have to say for it?*
> *Her brow grew bleak, her ancestors raged in their graves*
> *as she spoke with their ancient misery:*
> *'We'll pay for it, we'll pay for it, we'll pay for it!'*[9]

Sangharakshita speaks quite plainly in regard to this syndrome:

> If in your attempts to live a spiritual life you become anxious, make yourself wretched and insist on working yourself into a state of exhaustion something has clearly gone wrong.[10]

Coming from that tendency, when I first realized that opening to beauty and trying to manifest more beauty could be part of spiritual practice I was very excited. But then I realized that here was yet another challenge. It goes against the grain of our culture for a start. In our modern culture cynicism seems to be more acceptable. There's a deeper reason too (that perhaps the cynicism has grown out of). It can be frightening to open to beauty because it means going beyond the known and the familiar. It means going into the unknown and the unfamiliar, which usually makes us uncomfortable. There's a Buddhist story I like that illustrates this. A woman goes to the market in the next village with her basket full of fish to sell. She sells all her wares but realizes she's left it too late to get home to her own village. Her friend, the flower-seller, comes to her rescue and says she can sleep in her shop. Gratefully the woman lies down. But try as she might she can't get to sleep – the sweet smell of the flowers is keeping her awake. There's only one thing to do. She takes the smelly fish basket and puts it over her head, and with a sigh of relief she falls asleep.

Often we'd rather stay in our 'comfort zone', in the safe confines of what we know – even if the known is rather stale and smelly – rather than take the risk of stepping into new realms. In particular we can stifle our own positivity. You may suddenly feel like giving someone a gift when it's not even their birthday – but then the rationalization kicks in. You tell yourself, 'They'll think I want something back', or, 'We don't do that sort of thing in our family', until you end up with, 'It was a silly idea anyway.' In this way, you can easily talk yourself out of your own creative impulses. Repressing your positivity like this will have an impoverishing effect on you: it depresses you.

If acting in a beautiful way is challenging, then how much more so the notion of one's self and one's attributes simply 'being beautiful'. In British culture, one of the very worst things you can do is to 'show off' or 'stand out' – and woe betide you if you do; you'll soon hear the mutterings of, 'Who does she think she is?' Recently I heard a well-known poet being interviewed. She said she'd started writing and then publishing relatively late in life and that when she'd begun she'd met with a lot of encouragement. This encouragement lasted up to the point, she told us rather ruefully, when her books began to become bestsellers – and then it became quite a different story. It seemed like people were quite willing to encourage her as long as she didn't become more successful than themselves. I have an early memory of my own that's connected with this area. I was still at nursery school so I must have been about four, and I had dressed up my doll Susie with great care in a long white flowing outfit. My idea was to take her to nursery school for the other little girls to play with. I can still remember my excitement, imagining how delighted all the other girls would be. When Lesley Murphy, who was four-and-a-half, came to call, I eagerly showed her Susie in her finery. 'Your doll is lovely,' said Lesley primly, 'but you can't take her to nursery, you'll make the other children jealous.' I was devastated. I'd never heard the word 'jealous' before and I remember asking my mum and dad again and again what it meant, and the impossibility of them trying to explain it to me when I'd never yet experienced it as an emotion. Even though I couldn't understand what 'jealous' meant, I knew I'd made some sort of major mistake. For many years I tried to ensure I'd never again do anything that would make others jealous – tying myself in a lot of knots along the way.

The Buddhist approach is much more straightforward. It says that, if you're worried that by letting your own beauty shine you're in danger of setting yourself above others, or in danger of being conceited or boastful, all you need to do is keep opening to, and rejoicing in, everyone else's beauty as well. And, what's more, seeing the positive in others will tend to draw it forth, so by relating in this way you'll be creating a richer, more abundant world. So you could decide to actively practise rejoicing in others, whether it's about the colour combination of their outfit or their forbearance in a difficult situation, whether it's about the meal they cooked or their courage in speaking out against injustice.

More than anything else, what will create beauty is the practice of the positive precepts. Someone who is practising the positive precepts will appear very attractive. Gampopa makes the rapturous statement that they will be 'the most beautiful ornament, the centre of all joys'. I remember hearing someone talk about going to see Dhardo Rimpoche, one of Sangharakshita's teachers whom Sangharakshita regarded as a living Bodhisattva, that is someone truly practising for the benefit of all beings. A friend took photos of them together, which they showed her afterwards. She said she was astonished at the pictures. In the encounter Dhardo Rimpoche had appeared as vigorous and glowing. Now, in the photos, he looked elderly and frail. The photos were the literal truth, but the literal isn't necessarily the real.

Something similar to this would have happened in the case of the Buddha's monks. After he passed away, the Buddha's monks would have meditated on him, on his qualities, on the stories they remembered. He would have come to life, as it were, in their minds. A combination of their love and devotion towards him and his qualities would synthesize, and transformed images of the Buddha would arise in their minds, perhaps even more closely revealing the 'essence' of Buddhahood than the stories about his historical life. These would be images that personified unlimited human potential. In their mind's eye, in their hearts, they'd see the Buddha perhaps shining like gold, perhaps holding up a red lotus, perhaps with a thousand arms, each one bearing an implement to help living beings.

 Practice suggestion: acting on the positive

The next time you have a generous impulse, for example to buy someone a gift or card, or to give some money to charity, try acting on it unreservedly (as long as this will not cause harm to yourself, such as putting yourself in debt).

Afterwards, take some time to reflect on the experience.

- How did acting on your generous impulse make you feel about yourself?
- How did it make you feel in relation to the world at large?
- Are you going to continue this practice?
- If so, how long for?

Chapter eight

....

Beyond goodness

My friend was on retreat in the Spanish mountains, camping outside every night on the bare earth. The first night, lying inside her little tent, on her own, hearing the noises of all the creeping and crawling things outside, she was so frightened she couldn't sleep. When it came to the next night, she knew she'd have to do something to remedy the situation. She knew she needed all her strength for the trek ahead, so she couldn't afford to miss more sleep. When she told me what she did, I was taken aback. She dismantled her tent and slept in the open! 'I was lying on the inside, scared of what was outside,' she said, 'so I took the tent away and there was no inside and outside anymore!' Sure enough, free from the fear of what was outside, from then on she slept soundly! What she did was daring, inspired – and totally counter-intuitive. Our instinct, especially when we feel threatened, is to fortify our boundaries – or try to. But for my friend, freedom from fear came from doing the opposite. By dismantling the tent, she dismantled the notion of boundaries altogether.

Beyond self-clinging

This gives a hint about the way in which the Buddha saw that we can free ourselves from suffering. The Buddha's insight was that all our trouble, fear, and suffering is caused by clinging on to the idea of a fixed and separate 'me-in-here' while the rest of the world is 'out there'. We have an imperative then to try to protect that 'me' and spend most of our resources doing that. The Buddha realized that this is a futile mission that actually adds to our suffering. He realized that there is no fixed separate self to either cling to or do the clinging. So in fact it is only by letting go of that idea of a fixed and separate self, and therefore the need to protect it, that true

Reflection: whose will is it?

You'll need pen and paper.

Sit quietly, close your eyes, and spend one minute on each of these stages.

- Bring to mind, as vividly as you can, a recent time when someone asked you to do something (perhaps a small favour) and you *willingly* complied.
- Tune in to how bringing this to mind makes you feel physically.
- Tune in to how bringing this to mind makes you feel about yourself.
- Tune in to how responding as you did affected how you feel in relation to that person.
- Tune in to how you imagine responding as you did affected how that person feels in relation to you.
- Open your eyes and write three or four words about your experience of each of those stages.

happiness and liberation are found. We need to get over ourselves, to go beyond ourselves.

So you could say the Buddhist life is lived to transcend self-clinging. But this brings with it its own paradox. We're trying to transcend ourselves but we need to make a self-willed effort to do that. There is a real danger that our spiritual efforts actually deepen our self-clinging. Even though our self-clinging may become more refined, it can become stronger than ever. We're in danger of becoming like the rowan berry in another Norman MacCaig poem. The rowan berry begins by saying,

> *my cluster's the main one and I*
> *am the most important berry in it.*

Even knowing that it will be gobbled and deposited by a fieldfare, it manages to keep its sense of self-importance intact, albeit in a more subtle way, by imagining growing into a tree full of berries and becoming 'that fine thing, an ancestor'.[1] In other words we may have reflected deeply on the Buddhist teachings and even had some insight into the fact that we are not a fixed and separate self. The trouble is that we can become proud of that insight and to that extent we are not free of self-clinging after all.

In order to start exploring the way beyond this seeming paradox, try the reflective exercise on p.133, 'Whose will is it?' It will be particularly helpful to the exploration if you do this short reflection first, before reading on.

The first step in transcending self-clinging is to become more and more aware of yourself as an ethical agent. Then, as you resonate more and more deeply with others, you will tend to act more and more unselfishly. Whenever you do that, you will experience a lessening of the boundaries between yourself and other people. You've probably had the experience of someone you love asking you to do something and you responding by doing it – even doing it happily, willingly, delightedly. If you really love them you can feel more than happy to help. You might invite them to ask you for help, and really mean it. If you ask yourself in these instances, 'Whose will is operating?' you'll find you can't really say. You can't say it's totally their will because you're willingly doing it. But you can't say it's totally your will because they've asked you to do it. Your wills have become blended. And, as that happens, consciousness expands and the limiting sense of 'I' attenuates.

You can take this a step further by actively seeking to do the will of another, especially someone you look up to and regard as wiser than yourself. Sangharakshita deliberately sought to do the will of one of his own teachers, Jagdish Kashyap, precisely because he was aware of this inherent problem in the spiritual life – that is how to overcome the egoistic will with the will. Sangharakshita felt very strongly that even the practice of meditation would not be enough to overcome the momentum of the egoistic will. He needed something both more drastic and more down to earth, something that could be continually practised.[2] He practised like this in relation to his teacher in many small ways, and then finally, at the end of a trip to Kalimpong together, Jagdish Kashyap decided to enter into retreat and said to Sangharakshita, 'Stay here and work for the good of Buddhism.' Sangharakshita bowed his head in acquiescence. In fact all sorts of very positive things came out of that, but Sangharakshita couldn't

Not About Being Good

have predicted that at the time. At the time, he didn't feel experienced enough to work for Buddhism on his own, and wasn't sure what kind of reception he would get, but he had committed himself to doing what his teacher asked.[3] This obviously wasn't out of passive submission. His 'obedience' arose out of his receptivity to his teacher. Seeking to do the will of someone wise is not a matter of leaving your intelligence behind. It's more a matter of leaving your tendency to want things on your own terms behind. It's a deeply challenging practice. It will start to bite as soon as you are asked to do something you really don't want to do – or not to do something you really do want to do. You'll find yourself thinking, 'Yes, I know I said I'd do what you asked – but I didn't know you were going to ask me that!'

Challenging though that might be, if you really want to be free of self-clinging and so experience complete freedom from fear, ultimately you need to go even further than that. You need to be in contact with a dimension that goes completely beyond yourself. For Buddhists, this dimension is represented by the Buddha who himself went beyond all self-clinging. You can try to imagine the Buddha, imagine the mind of the Buddha. But in the end the Buddha is more than you can imagine. The scientist J.B.S. Haldane said:

> The universe is not only queerer than we suppose but queerer than
> we can suppose.[4]

We could say the mind of a Buddha is not only vaster than we suppose, but vaster than we can suppose. We have been exploring trying to discover who the Buddha is by trying to be like the Buddha. We have talked about opening to something that we experience as continually beyond ourselves. But because the Buddha is more than we can ever imagine, to really have a sense of the Buddha we need to have a sense of the Buddha reaching to us. Only this will enable us to actively blend our will with the will of the Buddha, the will to Enlightenment.

Again there is nothing passive about blending your will with the will of the Buddha, entrusting your will to the will of the Buddha. Surrendering your will to the will of the Buddha means you're surrendering your own limited needs and wants to the immense task of trying to liberate all beings from suffering. Usually the strongest, most primal urge within life is to preserve itself. Buddhist practice is leading you to a point where the will to Enlightenment becomes even stronger, even more primary than that. The will to Enlightenment then would have become the strongest urge within you. And if you are willing to set out on this journey then what will happen is the Buddha, as it were, will reach down and help you. Reality, so to speak, will be on your side and you'll discover that you are far more than you thought you were. In fact, if you want to go beyond yourself, it's essential that you feel your relationship with the Buddha as active, as dynamic, in this way.

Being lifted up

Throughout this book I've been saying that all the Buddhist teachings describe a natural process, verifiable by your own experience, or by the experience of the wise. In this section I want to explore how even the notion of the Buddha 'reaching down to help us' is part of this natural process, rather than the intrusion of something 'supernatural' that has to be taken on as an article of faith. I'll explore this by going through some analogies.

We all know what a positive effect it has to be encouraged by other people. I was fortunate enough to be a spectator at the Paralympics in London in 2012 on the night of the athletics finals. There was an amazing atmosphere with a full stadium cheering. This culminated in unrestrainable cries of 'Pea-cock! Pea-cock!' as the British runner Jonathan Peacock took his position on the starting blocks for the 100m sprint, which he won in 10.9s. Again and again, not just on that night, but during the whole of the Olympics and Paralympics, the British winners were saying, 'It was the crowd. I couldn't have done it without its support. It was the crowd who did it.' I was struck by the fact that they weren't just saying it was nice to have the crowd. They were saying that we, the crowd, actually had a crucial role. They were saying that they couldn't have done it without us. Of course we, the crowd, knew it was the athletes who'd done it really – but at the same time, from my own modest experience of running the Cumbernauld 10k, I knew what they meant. It really does seem that the people cheering you on – in my case from bus stops and doorsteps – are keeping you going. At the same time as knowing that I was the one literally running the race, I definitely found reserves of strength and energy I didn't know I had from the support. Others believed in me, others were willing me on, so I believed in myself. It was a very tangible experience. And it's commonplace enough. But what's really happening in that kind of experience, if you think about it, is not easy to pin down. Again there's a kind of blending of wills. Yes, I was being cheered on as I panted my way round the track, but for it to have an effect I had to allow the support in, to allow myself to be carried along, to be lifted up.

I now want to explore this phenomenon of allowing ourselves to be lifted up with a more subtle example. While I've been writing this book, I've been thinking about my father. In a way the book is dedicated to him. My father has been dead for over ten years. I know that he, from his working-class background, would have been inordinately proud that his daughter had written a book. Not only that, but just before he died he started to get interested in Buddhism. In fact he had the *Dhammapada* – the words of the Buddha – in hospital with him during his last days. I think he would have been very interested in many of the ideas I'm doing my best to express. And thinking of that inspires me to try to express them the very best I can. Again it's a tangible experience. But what does this mean? What does it mean to be inspired by someone who's died? Obviously he is never going to see, read, or even know about this book. What does it even mean to use the word 'he' anymore? I don't imagine him on some cloud smiling fondly down at me. Yet, still, the experience of the very best in me being drawn out by the notion I'm dedicating it to him has a truth that seems to go beyond the literal. Again it's not an uncommon experience to feel like we're receiving encouragement, even advice, from someone who isn't physically there, even who isn't physically alive. There's a definite experience, but that experience doesn't correspond to any 'thing' that we can find. Then again, that's actually, according to Buddhism, true of all experience; there is experience but it doesn't map onto any fixed, unchanging 'things'. And according to Buddhism the more deeply we know this the more we will have insight into the true nature of reality. We can start the process of this deeper knowing by reflecting that the physical waking world – the world we tend to call the 'real' world – isn't the only reality. There is also reality in the world of dreams, meditations, imagination (or perhaps it's more accurate to say that all these worlds are just as 'real' as they are 'unreal'). At the same time, connecting with all these realms doesn't require us to believe in any 'supernatural' agent. It's entirely natural.

We can look to the artistic process for even more subtlety. Every week a group of us bring poems for feedback to my poetry teacher. She looks not so much at the poem we've written but at the poem our poem is trying to be. She is trying to teach us to look in this way. What she sees in our poems can seem so 'right' that it feels more like a magical display than the masterclass it is. But it's not that she has some mystic psychic powers that will be forever beyond the rest of us. She's 'simply' supremely gifted in the art of tuning in to the poem, letting it speak to her, as it were, and listening to it. She's trying to help us to learn how to discover the 'real' poem that is trying to emerge through our fledgling efforts. It's hard to quite put into words what that really means. It's not as if 'the real poem' is literally out there in all its completeness waiting to be netted like a butterfly. Yet, when we do find it, it may well seem like that: it can feel so 'right' that it's as if it was there waiting. It feels like the poem will direct you to itself if you can learn to be sensitive enough to recognize it. In the poem 'Makings', Maitreyabandhu describes a similar phenomenon in painting. The 'maker' is painting a picture of his father, and then:

> You were altering
> the jaw line, very slightly, with the tip
> of a filbert brush, when there he was!
> your father looking up at you and smiling.[5]

It can happen with anything creative we do. Recently, making a Buddhist shrine, I'd arranged flowers, candles, cloths. It looked alright – it would serve the purpose – but it wasn't really alive. Then on an inspiration I put some oranges in a golden bowl and placed them on the shrine. Instantly it was as if the shrine came alive and looked back at me, glowing, and spoke to me: 'Yes, that's it, I'm complete now.' The addition of the oranges changed everything. It wasn't 'old-shrine-plus-oranges'. It was suddenly completely new. My only 'job' was to be receptive to that. Not to suddenly impose my small will. Not to spoil it.

I've taken some time over these analogies because I'm sure that to some extent, and in some form, they will feel familiar to you.

They may be just faint echoes, but the experiences I've tried to evoke of being drawn on by something that is apparently outside yourself are essentially no different from the experience that will be felt as the Buddha reaching down to you. They are essentially no different from the experience that will be felt as a force that emerges within consciousness that carries you beyond individual selfhood. You can practise learning to be alert to this phenomenon of being drawn on, being lifted up, at all levels. And whenever you do experience it you can practise 'getting out of the way' and allowing the mysterious to unfold within you.

We can understand this material in terms of the niyamas, those natural laws governing the relationships between conditions and their effects that we met back in Chapter 1. These were the natural laws the first three of which govern inorganic matter, organic life, and simple consciousness, including instincts. The fourth is the law of karma, which is that the consequences of an action are appropriate to the volitional impulse behind it, and which in one way or another has been the subject matter of this book so far. Fifthly, there is the natural law that means human beings can become Buddhas – Dharma-niyama. Dharma-niyama processes, then, are those conditioned processes that mean Buddhas can arise. You can see that the processes these laws govern are in an ascending order of complexity. It's the last two sets of processes, those governed by the karma-niyama and those governed by the Dharma-niyama, that are relevant to the spiritual life – in fact that make the spiritual life possible. And all these laws are natural. They are 'laws of nature'. Some lines of a poem by Don Paterson go:

> But the target also draws our aim –
> our will and nature's are the same;
> we are its living word and not
> a book it wrote and then forgot[6]

So he's saying everything in nature, including ourselves, has the urge to transcend itself. And not only that, but 'the target also draws our aim.' Sometimes it will feel as if we're being drawn on, we're being helped. Don Paterson is a self-declared scientific materialist who believes 'there's no-one here but us chickens', so you can be sure he is not positing anything 'other-worldly' here. So again I'll emphasize that we don't have to either. Although, of course, the significant difference between a Buddhist world view and a scientific-materialist one is that Buddhism does not limit this process of transcendence to the material world, and, as we saw in Chapter 5, the views that we have condition the very way in which these processes unfold within us.

Karma-niyama and Dharma-niyama

Although all human beings have the potential to become Buddhas, not all of them do so. Enlightenment isn't a random event, nor is it a given. Even though everything in nature has that urge for transcendence, it doesn't always manage to successfully fulfil that urge. As a matter of fact, even calling it 'the urge for transcendence' may be putting it a bit too grandiosely. I remember seeing a cartoon of a woman shopping – the caption read, 'I don't know what I want, but I know I won't be happy until I get it.' This is perhaps a better description of the state we find ourselves in. Buddhism doesn't 'blame' us for being in that state, and doesn't put forward a 'first cause' for it. Buddhism simply describes for us the conditions that will lead us from that state of dissatisfaction to a state of satisfaction, fulfilment, and meaning. The law of karma means that, if you act self-centredly, that is if you try to organize reality to suit yourself with no care for others, then sooner or later you will run into frustration. To the extent that you act in the ways that Buddhism defines as skilful, you won't run into obstruction so you won't meet with frustration. The Buddhist path is not something prescriptive to be draped over our lives like a constraining garment. Rather it is simply a description of the conditions that lead to fulfilment. And all you're doing in following the Buddhist path is cooperating with those conditions.

If you do cooperate with the conditions that lead to fulfilment, not only will you not run into obstruction, you will in fact feel 'drawn on'. What we have called Dharma-niyama processes will feel as if they are coming from beyond your individual will. They will feel like something that is carrying you onward and upward – remembering all the time that these notions of 'individual will' and 'beyond the

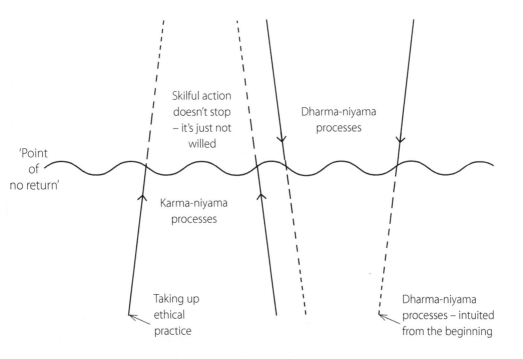

'Point
of
no return'

Skilful action
doesn't stop
– it's just not
willed

Dharma-niyama
processes

Karma-niyama
processes

Taking up
ethical
practice

Dharma-niyama
processes – intuited
from the beginning

Fig. 5: Dharma-niyama and karma-niyama processes in relation to each other

individual will' are only provisional operational concepts. In our unenlightened state, it's impossible not to think of things existing either 'in here' – that is within our own minds – or 'out there' in the universe. But by continually practising to become less and less selfish at the same time as intentionally opening up to dimensions beyond the individual will, in the end the notions of something existing 'in here' or 'out there' will break down. They will prove to be equally true – or untrue.

Figure 5 is a diagram I've found helpful in showing how dharma-niyama processes and karma-niyama processes are in relation to each other.[7] Imagine the karma-niyama processes as something ascending – like a space rocket trying to launch itself – and the Dharma-niyama processes as something descending – like the gravity field of a far-off planet that the rocket is trying to fly to. The karma-niyama processes start reaching upwards, as it were, when we begin to act more and more skilfully. The law of karma means that, when we do that, consciousness emerges in more and more subtle and refined forms, and expands beyond a narrow self-reference. Self-clinging becomes weakened. The more the tendency to self-reference weakens, the more a new process can come into play: progress in accordance with the Dharma-niyama, which is independent of selfish volition, that is, independent of the tendency to try and organize reality to suit ourselves. Figure 5 shows how the processes governed by the Dharma-niyama can be intuited right at the beginning of our spiritual journey and then their influence becomes stronger, then gradually starts to take over, then takes over altogether. When that happens, Dharma-niyama processes spontaneously unfold in more and more rich and satisfying forms, increasingly replacing the old self-referential willing. There is still a motivation, but it's coming less and less from the individual will, it's not just serving the interests of that individual.

This altruistic motivating force will feel like it is a will from beyond your own will, that carries you onward and upward. If you align yourself with it, cooperate with it, finally all that will be left will be spontaneous compassionate activity. There will be no 'I' any more, no agent anymore, so karma will have been transcended altogether. You will have become 'trackless', as one of the epithets for the Buddha describes him. Another way of putting this is that you will no longer have to practise skilful action; what we – unenlightened – call skilful action or compassion is simply the expression of an Enlightened state. Someone who is manifesting perfect wisdom doesn't have to try to act kindly or try to speak truthfully; those actions will be a natural expression of that realization. Genuine compassion isn't something sentimental – in fact it isn't even an emotion at all. An Enlightened being would see a need and simply respond to that. In a certain sense you could say that an Enlightened being has no choice but to act and speak in this way.

Figure 5 also shows 'the point of no return'. This is when your spiritual momentum has reached the point where there's no falling back. Going back to the analogy of the rocket, you could say that it is now at the point where the gravitational field of the far-distant planet has more influence than the gravitational field of the earth. Spiritually speaking, it's the point where you recognize that self-clinging has no validity. Even though you can't yet stop it as a habitual tendency – that will happen at full Enlightenment – it can't take hold of you, it can't dominate. You can no longer build a life on selfishness. You can no longer build a life on the basis of unskilfulness – that is why someone who has reached this point, although they may still act unskilfully in subtle ways, will instantly confess. It's a decisive point where you are now drawn on by an unwavering conviction that there is experience beyond self-clinging. This insight now 'takes the place' of the practice of making sure you're in conditions where you can sustain your ethical practice. No conditions, no matter how difficult, can ever overturn your conviction again.

Sangharakshita has said that this 'point of no return' where you enter the 'stream of the Dharma' – or indeed when it enters you – is attainable by any serious practitioner in their lifetime. At the same time, he has stressed that this can never be 'my' achievement. In other words, you need to be careful that you don't become so focused on this as a goal that you deny the possibility of it. You need to feel that you are engaging with spiritual life not just for yourself or you will – perhaps without realizing it – be catapulted back into ego-clinging. The spirit of self-transcendence can't be complete without the collective. The healthy thing is to put yourself into the service of creating a culture where it is natural for everybody to grow. In that way, you will be giving up your individual will to something more than your individual will and simply trying to create the circumstances in which the spirit of self-transcendence arises and where it doesn't matter in whom.

Beyond Buddhism

It's important to remember that everything we talk about being receptive to as a means to go beyond ego-clinging – whether we call it Buddhahood, Enlightenment, Dharma-niyama processes – is a metaphor. Words can't keep up with the spiritual realities. In fact our mundane minds can't keep up with the spiritual realities. If we feel the touch of something 'beyond' we'll tend to reify it, which, by solidifying it, contaminates it once again with ego-clinging. But Buddhism specifically encourages, even instructs, us not to do that. It encourages us to be open to the experience and be open to the mystery of it. Buddhism, in fact, is constantly trying to point us beyond Buddhism.

Since we have now gone almost beyond words, certainly beyond the literal, I wanted to end by returning to poetry. In Chapter 7 we left the foal in Ted Hughes' poem

> *Pretending each day more and more Horse*
> *Till he's perfect Horse.*

If you don't know the poem, you could be forgiven for thinking that it ends here with the foal becoming 'perfect Horse'. After all, what more is there to say after that? But in fact that's not the end. Here's how the poem goes on.

> *Then unearthly Horse*
> *Will surge through him, weightless, a spinning of flame*
> *Under sudden gusts.*
> *It will coil his eyeball and his heel*
> *In a single terror – like the awe*
> *Between lightning and thunderclap.*[8]

It's as if becoming 'perfect Horse' has been the necessary preparation for something from another dimension entirely, for 'unearthly Horse' to descend and totally transform the foal. The fact that its eyeball and heel are coiled 'in a single terror' shows that this experience is shocking; everything 'known' is burnt up, blown away, and a new realm is entered, infinitely vaster.

To me this poem gives a hint as to what our practice of ethics is really about – or can really be about if we want it to. First of all, as a result of skilful practice your sensibilities are amplified, extended, refined. You become more and more alive to things. You become more willing to let go of your old self, and to open to the new – even give yourself up to it. You become more and more truly human. And all this preparation means you will be ready for something that you will feel as a force coming from beyond yourself and that, if you

Fig. 6: The Buddha

allow yourself to go with it, will carry you on to greater and greater fulfilment.

And all of this is a completely natural process. The capacity for Enlightenment is part of the way things are. Just as apples fall to the ground, human beings can become Buddhas.

Reflection: receptivity to the Buddha

The last suggestion for reflection is an exercise in receptivity; it is taking the reflection in Chapter 7 a stage further.

Sit comfortably, in an upright position with your eyes closed. Connect with a sense of your weight dropping down into the floor and into the cushions or chair.

Now tune in to the natural flow of your breath, just following that with your attention.

Now imagine that you are sitting in the presence of the Buddha, who is also sitting still and meditating. Allow the sense of presence of the Buddha to steady and deepen. You could reflect that the Buddha taught and practised this Mindfulness of Breathing.

Continue to sit, aware of your breath and aware of the presence of the Buddha for five minutes (or longer if you want to).

Now tune in to the effect that sitting in the presence of the Buddha is having on *you*. Is there even a teaching for you?

Then relax your imaginative efforts but sit still for another minute or so to absorb the effects of meditation.

Notes and references

Introduction

1 I have particularly drawn on a seminar given by Sangharakshita in 1980 on 'The perfection of ethics and manners', chapter 13 of *The Jewel Ornament of Liberation*, by Gampopa.

2 J.M. Coetzee, *Disgrace*, Vintage, London 2000, p.89.

3 Iain Crichton Smith, 'The law and the grace', in *Twentieth-Century Scottish Poetry*, ed. Douglas Dunn, Faber and Faber, London 1993, p.253.

4 *The New Shorter Oxford English Dictionary*, 4th edition, Oxford University Press, Oxford 1993, vol. 1, p.857.

5 See Subhuti, 'Remorse and confession in the spiritual community', essay available at www.subhuti.info, accessed on 10 April 2013.

6 Ibid.

7 Article in *The Big Issue*, 2 July 2012. 'Faith' in Buddhism has no connotations of 'blind faith'. Rather, it is something more like confidence or trust. 'Buddha-Dharma' here means the teachings of Buddhism.

8 Tassajara is a Zen Buddhist meditation centre, set in the mountains in California.

9 Edward Espe Brown, *The Complete Tassajara Cookbook*, Shambhala Publications, Boston and London 2009, p.x.

Chapter 1: Doing it for you

1 Śāntideva, *The Bodhicaryāvatāra*, trans. Kate Crosby and Andrew Skilton, Oxford University Press, Oxford 1996, chapter 6, verse 107, p.107.

2 Maitreyabandhu, *Life with Full Attention*, Windhorse Publications, Cambridge 2009, p.37.

3 The niyamas, and their origins in Buddhaghosa's writing, are described in detail in 'Revering and Relying Upon the Dharma' by Subhuti and Sangharakshita, at http://subhuti.info/sites/subhuti.info/files/revering_and_relying_upon_the_dharma.pdf, accessed on 12 December 2014. See also Sangharakshita, *What is the Dharma?*, Windhorse Publications, 1998, pp.164–5.

4 Lekha Sutta, *Aṅguttara Nikāya* i.283 in *The Numerical Discourses of the Buddha: A Translation of the Aṅguttara Nikāya* 132 (10) trans. Bhikkhu Bodhi, Wisdom, Boston 2012, pp.361-2.

5 I got this idea from a talk given by Subhuti to members of the Triratna Buddhist Order in 2011.

Chapter 2: Doing it for others

1 *Dhammapada* 1-2, trans. Sangharakshita, Windhorse Publications, Birmingham 2001, p.13.

2 *Dhammapada*, trans. Ṭhānissaro Bhikkhu, Dhamma Dana Publications, Barre 1998, p.137; quoted in Ratnaguna, *The Art of Reflection*, Windhorse Publications, Cambridge 2010, p.93.

3 Sangharakshita, *The Three Jewels*, Windhorse Publications, Purley 1977, p.112.

4 Martin Amis, *God's Dice*, Penguin, London 1995, p.23.

5 Sangharakshita, *The Ten Pillars of Buddhism*, 5th edition, Windhorse Publications, Cambridge 2010, p.67.

6 *The Compact Oxford English Dictionary*, op. cit., p.850, my italics.

7 Sangharakshita, *Transforming Self and World*, Windhorse Publications, Birmingham 1995, p.209.

8 This exercise could in theory be done with something you enjoy about someone else's behaviour, but you are much less likely to stop and want to reflect when things are going your way.

9 Śāntideva, *The Bodhicaryāvatāra*, op. cit., chapter 8, verse 129, p.99.

10 Penelope Fitzgerald, *Offshore, Human Voices, The Beginning of Spring*, Everyman's Library, London 2003, p.280.

11 Gampopa, *The Jewel Ornament of Liberation*, trans. and annotated by Herbert V. Guenther, Rider and Company, London 1970, p.163.

12 Percy Bysshe Shelley, in *A Defence of Poetry and Other Essays*, written in 1821, available at http://www.gutenberg.org/files/5428/5428-h/5428-h. htm#link2H_4_0010, accessed on 26 April 2013.

13 See Sangharakshita, *Living with Kindness*, Windhorse Publications, Birmingham 2004, p.97.

14 Ibid., p.98.

15 Sangharakshita, *Mind Reactive and Creative*, Windhorse Publications, Birmingham 1995, p.11.

16 Saṃsāra isn't, as it's sometimes spoken of, a place. Rather it means to go round and round. It's something we do; we 'samsarize'.

17 John Burnside, *A Lie about My Father*, Jonathan Cape, London 2006, p.252.

Chapter 3: Doing something that works

1   Edward Espe Brown, *The Complete Tassajara Cookbook*, op. cit., p.x.
2   Aṅgulimāla Sutta, *Majjhima Nikāya* 86. You can find this in *The Middle Length Discourses of the Buddha: A New Translation of the Majjhima Nikāya*, trans. Bhikkhu Ñāṇamoli and Bhikkhu Bodhi, Wisdom, Boston 1995, pp.710-717.
3   This story is told in *Mahāvagga* viii.26 of the Vinaya Piṭaka. See also Sangharakshita, *The Buddha's Victory*, Windhorse Publications, Glasgow 1991, chapter 4, 'A Case of Dysentery'.
4   The story of Kisagotami is told in Mrs C.A.F Rhys Davids and K. Norman (trans.), *Poems of Early Buddhist Nuns (Therīgāthā)*, Pali Text Society, Oxford 1997, pp.88-91.
5   There seems to be a supernatural phenomenon happening when Aṅgulimāla cannot keep up with the Buddha, but its place in the story, I'd suggest, is to serve the main point being communicated, rather than being itself the main point.
6   John 11:1–46, *King James Bible*.
7   Saki, H.H. Munro, 'The storyteller', in *The Best of Saki*, Orion Publishing Group, London 1995, p.149.
8   Someone who has dedicated their lives to the attainment of Enlightenment for the sake of all beings.
9   'He will wear his righteousness as lightly as a flower. He will never make of it a whip for the backs of the unrighteous.' Sangharakshita, *A Survey of Buddhism*, 9th edition, Windhorse Publications, Birmingham 2001, p.480.
10 Irène Némirovsky, *Suite Française*, Vintage, London 2007, p.13.
11 I got the notion of 'pseudo-spiritualism' from a talk given by Vessantara to members of the Triratna Buddhist Community (formerly the Friends of the Western Buddhist Order).
12 For example, if you've cultivated irritation previously, this will make it more likely to be your knee-jerk response to an unpleasant stimulus.
13 See Padmavajra, *Training in the Ten Precepts*, Padmaloka Books, Padmaloka 1996, p.5.

Chapter 4: A guide for living

1   *Dialogues of the Buddha*, part 1, trans. T.W. Rhys Davids, Pali Text Society, reprinted London 1956, p.179; quoted in Sangharakshita, *The Ten Pillars of Buddhism*, op. cit., p.19.
2   *The Book of Gradual Sayings (Aṅguttara Nikāya)*, vol. 5, trans. F.L. Woodward, Pali Text Society, reprinted London 1972, pp.178–80; quoted in Sangharakshita, ibid., p.24.
3   *Collins Concise Dictionary*, HarperCollins, Glasgow 1995, p.1084.
4   Seminars make mention of this from about 1975, seven years after Triratna (then the FWBO) was founded.

5 Although the five dharmas are not found in the Buddhist scriptures as such, all the positive qualities that the positive precepts cover can be found in the scriptures.

6 The set of ten precepts adds three more speech precepts to the set of five precepts, and introduces three new mind precepts. Also, the fifth precept from the set of five precepts – covering abstention from intoxicants and developing mindfulness – is not included in the ten precepts. This is because, for people putting the ten precepts into practice in their lives, it is generally understood that they will also know of the five precepts, and so will include the fifth of these in their ethical practice. This makes a total of eleven precepts, and those following the ten precepts implicitly undertake to practice all eleven.

7 Kahlil Gibran, *The Prophet*, William Heinemann Ltd, London 1980, p.27.

8 Don Paterson, 'Phantom', in *Rain*, Faber and Faber, London 2011, p.51.

9 Śāntideva, *The Bodhicaryāvatāra*, op. cit., chapter 3, verse 11, p.21.

10 Adapted from a reflection in Paramananda, *A Deeper Beauty*, Windhorse Publications, Birmingham 2003, p.26.

11 Richard Holloway, *Godless Morality*, Canongate Books Ltd, Edinburgh 2005, p.43.

12 Norman MacCaig, 'Walking home exhausted', in *The Poems of Norman MacCaig*, ed. Ewen McCaig, Polygon, Edinburgh 2005, p.173.

13 This interview is still available to watch on YouTube at https://www.youtube.com/watch?v=NoevVtG-Gh8.

14 Sangharakshita, *The Ten Pillars of Buddhism*, op. cit., p.103.

15 That is, the spiritual community.

16 Ratnaghosha, 'A word of magic', talk available at http://ratnaghosa.fwbo.net/wordfive.html, accessed on 15 April 2013.

17 Abhayarājakumāra Sutta, *Majjhima Nikāya* 58. See *The Middle Length Discourses of the Buddha*, op. cit., pp.498-501.

18 This idea was inspired by Maitreyabandhu, *Life with Full Attention*, op. cit., p.202.

19 Ibid., p.111.

20 *Dhammapada* 336, trans. Sangharakshita, op. cit., p.113.

21 Ibid., verse 5, p.14.

22 Sangharakshita, *The Ten Pillars of Buddhism*, op. cit., p.118.

23 Sangharakshita, *Know Your Mind*, Windhorse Publications, Birmingham 1998, p.181.

24 *Dīgha Nikāya* 1. See *The Long Discourses of the Buddha: A Translation of the Dīgha Nikāya*, trans. Maurice Walshe, Wisdom, Boston 1995, pp.67-90.

25 Sangharakshita, *Living with Kindness*, op. cit., p.134.

26 *The Book of Gradual Sayings*, op. cit., p.178; quoted in Sangharakshita, *The Ten Pillars of Buddhism*, op. cit., p.119.

27 Ibid., p.119.

28 Sangharakshita, *Living with Kindness*, op. cit., p.136.

29 Ibid., p.134.

Chapter 5: A deeper motivation

1 Robert Browning, 'Andrea del Sarto', in *The Norton Anthology of Poetry*, Norton, New York 2005, p.1034.
2 Sangharakshita, *Peace is a Fire*, 2nd edition, Windhorse Publications, Birmingham 1995, p.18.
3 Robert Burns, 'Tam O'Shanter', in *A Choice of Burns's Poems and Songs*, introduced by Sydney Goodsir Smith, Faber and Faber, London 1966, p.60.
4 See Sangharakshita, *Know Your Mind*, op. cit., p.146 and Mahāparinibbāna Sutta, *Dīgha Nikāya* 15 in Maurice Walshe (trans.), *The Long Discourses of the Buddha*, op. cit., p.270.
5 See Sangharakshita, *Know Your Mind*, op. cit., p.147.
6 Sangharakshita, *The Ten Pillars of Buddhism*, op. cit., p.16.
7 Seamus Heaney, 'Saw music', in *District and Circle*, Faber and Faber, London 2006, p.50.
8 Appaṭivāṇa Sutta, *Aṅguttara Nikāya* (i.50) translation by Ṭhānissaro Bhikkhu, available at http://www.accesstoinsight.org/tipitaka/an/an02/an02.005. than.html, accessed on 15 April 2013. You can find a slightly different translation in Bhikkhu Bodhi's *The Numerical Discourses of the Buddha*, 5 (5), op.cit., pp.141-2.
9 Chase Twichell, 'Weightless like a River', in *The Snow Watcher*, Ontario Review Press, San Francisco 1998.

Chapter 6: Learning to die

1 Oscar Wilde, *The Picture of Dorian Gray*, Penguin, London 2003, p.94.
2 Sangharakshita, *Transforming Self and World*, Windhorse Publications, Birmingham 1995, p.88.
3 Richard Holloway, *Godless Morality*, op. cit., p.5.
4 Sangharakshita, *The Inconceivable Emancipation*, Windhorse Publications, Birmingham 1995, p.74.
5 At least I've noticed it as such in the UK and Ireland.
6 'The threefold pūja', in *Puja: The Triratna Book of Buddhist Devotional Texts*, Windhorse Publications, Cambridge 2012, p.34.
7 See Sangharakshita, *The Inconceivable Emancipation*, op. cit., p.75.
8 This meditation practice is called the Mettā Bhāvanā or 'development of universal loving-kindness'.
9 'Healing perspective', *Dharma Life* 19, available at www.dharmalife.com/ issue19/people.html, accessed on 26 April 2013.
10 Ratnaghosha, 'The helpful enemy', in *Kṣānti*, booklet printed by the London Buddhist Centre, 1997, p.24.

Chapter 7: Being reborn

1 Gampopa, *The Jewel Ornament of Liberation*, op. cit., p.164.
2 Sangharakshita, *A Survey of Buddhism*, Tharpa Publications, London 1987, p.167.
3 Ted Hughes, 'New Foal', in *Ted Hughes: Poems Selected by Simon Armitage*, Faber and Faber, London 2000, p.83.
4 *The Compact Oxford English Dictionary*, op. cit., p.1424.
5 Available at www.thinkexist.com, accessed on 15 April 2013.
6 Norman MacCaig, 'July evening', op. cit., p.116.
7 Tomas Tranströmer, 'Romanesque arches', trans. Robert Bly, in *The Half-Finished Heaven: The Best Poems of Tomas Tranströmer*, Gray Wolf Press, Minneapolis 2001.
8 Mahāgosiṅga Sutta, *Majjhima Nikāya* 32. See *The Middle Length Discourses of the Buddha: A New Translation of the Majjhima Nikāya*, op.cit., pp.307-12.
9 Alastair Reid, 'Scotland', in *Twentieth-Century Scottish Poetry*, ed. Douglas Dunn, Polygon Books, Edinburgh.
10 Sangharakshita, *Living Ethically*, Windhorse Publications, Cambridge 2009, p.126.

Chapter 8: Beyond goodness

1 Norman MacCaig, 'Rowan berry', op. cit., p.351.
2 Sangharakshita, *In the Sign of the Golden Wheel*, Windhorse Publications, Birmingham 1996, p.449.
3 Ibid., p.456.
4 Quote from J.B.S. Haldane, available at http://www.economist.com/node/922185, accessed on 25 April 2013.
5 Maitreyabandhu, 'Makings', in *The Bond*, Smith/Doorstop Books, Sheffield 2011, p.11.
6 Don Paterson, 'The circle', in *Rain*, op. cit., p.10.
7 A version of this diagram was used in a talk given by Ratnadharini to members of the Triratna Buddhist Order in 2010.
8 Ted Hughes, 'New Foal', op. cit., p.83.

Index

WINDHORSE PUBLICATIONS

Windhorse Publications is a Buddhist charitable company based in the UK. We place great emphasis on producing books of high quality that are accessible and relevant to those interested in Buddhism at whatever level. We are the main publisher of the works of Sangharakshita, the founder of the Triratna Buddhist Order and Community. Our books draw on the whole range of the Buddhist tradition, including translations of traditional texts, commentaries, books that make links with contemporary culture and ways of life, biographies of Buddhists, and works on meditation.

As a not-for-profit enterprise, we ensure that all surplus income is invested in new books and improved production methods, to better communicate Buddhism in the 21st century. We welcome donations to help us continue our work – to find out more, go to windhorsepublications.com.

The Windhorse is a mythical animal that flies over the earth carrying on its back three precious jewels, bringing these invaluable gifts to all humanity: the Buddha (the 'awakened one'), his teaching, and the community of all his followers.

Windhorse Publications
38 Newmarket Road
Cambridge CB5 8DT
UK
info@windhorsepublications.com

Consortium Book Sales & Distribution
210 American Drive
Jackson TN 38301
USA

Windhorse Books
PO Box 574
Newtown NSW 2042
Australia

THE TRIRATNA BUDDHIST COMMUNITY

Windhorse Publications is a part of the Triratna Buddhist Community, an international movement with centres in Europe, India, North and South America and Australasia. At these centres, members of the Triratna Buddhist Order offer classes in meditation and Buddhism. Activities of the Triratna Community also include retreat centres, residential spiritual communities, ethical Right Livelihood businesses, and the Karuna Trust, a UK fundraising charity that supports social welfare projects in the slums and villages of India.

Through these and other activities, Triratna is developing a unique approach to Buddhism, not simply as a philosophy and a set of techniques, but as a creatively directed way of life for all people living in the conditions of the modern world.

If you would like more information about Triratna please visit thebuddhistcentre.com or write to:

London Buddhist Centre
51 Roman Road
London E2 0HU
UK

Aryaloka
14 Heartwood Circle
Newmarket NH 03857
USA

Sydney Buddhist Centre
24 Enmore Road
Sydney NSW 2042
Australia

Also from Windhorse Publications

Living Ethically
Advice from Nagarjuna's Precious Garland

by Sangharakshita

In a world of increasingly confused ethics, *Living Ethically* looks back over the centuries for guidance from Nagarjuna, one of the greatest teachers of the Mahayana tradition. Drawing on the themes of Nagarjuna's famous scripture, *Precious Garland of Advice for a King*, this book explores the relationship between an ethical lifestyle and the development of wisdom. Covering both personal and collective ethics, Sangharakshita considers such enduring themes as pride, power and business, as well as friendship, love and generosity.

Sangharakshita is the founder of the Triratna Buddhist Community, a worldwide Buddhist movement. He has a lifetime of teaching experience and is the author of over 40 books.

ISBN 9781 899579 86 0
£11.99 / $17.95 / €15.95
216 pages

Living Wisely
Further Advice from Nagarjuna's Precious Garland

by Sangharakshita

How do we live wisely? This is the burning question that Sangharakshita seeks to answer in this companion volume of commentary on a famous text, *Precious Garland of Advice for a King*, the advice being that of the great Indian Buddhist teacher Nagarjuna. In the companion volume, *Living Ethically*, Sangharakshita showed us that to live a Buddhist life we need to develop an ethical foundation, living in a way that is motivated increasingly by love, contentment and awareness. However, from a Buddhist viewpoint, 'being good' is not good enough. We need to use our positive ethical position, our momentum in goodness, to develop wisdom, a deep understanding of the true nature of existence. We become good in order to learn to be wise.

Sangharakshita is the founder of the Triratna Buddhist Community, a worldwide Buddhist movement. He has a lifetime of teaching experience and is the author of over 40 books.

ISBN 9781 907314 93 3
£10.99 / $16.95 / €13.95
152 pages

Buddhist Wisdom in Practice **series**

The Art of Reflection

by Ratnaguna

It is all too easy either to think obsessively, or to not think enough. But how do we think usefully? How do we reflect? Like any art, reflection can be learnt and developed, leading to a deeper understanding of life and to the fullness of wisdom. *The Art of Reflection* is a practical guide to reflection as a spiritual practice, about 'what we think and how we think about it'. It is a book about contemplation and insight, and reflection as a way to discover the truth.

No-one who takes seriously the study and practice of the Dharma should fail to read this ground-breaking book. – Sangharakshita, founder of the Triratna Buddhist Community

ISBN 9781 899579 89 1
£9.99 / $16.95 / €12.95
160 pages

This Being, That Becomes

by Dhivan Thomas Jones

Dhivan Thomas Jones takes us into the heart of the Buddha's insight that everything arises in dependence on conditions. With the aid of lucid reflections and exercises he prompts us to explore how conditionality works in our own lives, and provides a sure guide to the most essential teaching of Buddhism.

Clearly and intelligently written, this book carries a lot of good advice. – Prof Richard Gombrich, author of *What the Buddha Thought*

ISBN 9781 899579 90 7
£10.99 / $15.95 / €13.95
216 pages

A Buddhist View series

Finding the Mind

by Robin Cooper

'Here am I, in this body I call my own, among millions that are mysteriously other. What's going on?' You may have asked this, or something like it, at some point in your life. How can you find the answer?

Buddhism points to your own mind as a way to understand and transform your experience. But, as Robin Cooper explains, it takes an exploratory approach, it asks you to seek: it is not a revelation of religious truths. The Buddha saw that we are all in a tough predicament. We are constantly anxious about what we lack and what we may lose, and in chasing security we easily cause pain to others. But the Buddha did not offer to save us through faith in his truth. Instead, he asked us to explore. Be aware, probe the edges of your awareness, investigate, and find your mind.

ISBN 9781 9073140 3 2
£6.99 / $14.95 / € 10.95
160 pages

Solitude and Loneliness

by Sarvananda

Charlie Chaplin observed, 'Loneliness is the theme of everyone.' Although true, it is equally true that we all very skillfully, and often unconsciously, organize our lives in such a way as to avoid loneliness.

Drawing on a wide range of sources – the poets Dickinson and Hafiz, the painter Edward Hopper, the sage Milarepa, the lives of Helen Keller and Chris McCandless, and of course the Buddha – Sarvananda explores the themes of isolation, loneliness and solitude from a Buddhist perspective and examines how and why our relationship to ourselves can be a source of both suffering and liberation.

ISBN 9781 907314 07 0
£8.99 / $14.95 / €10.95
152 pages

Introducing Mindfulness: Buddhist Background and Practical Exercises

by Bhikkhu Anālayo

Buddhist meditator and scholar Bhikkhu Anālayo introduces the Buddhist background to mindfulness practice, from mindful eating to its formal cultivation as satipaṭṭhāna (the foundations of mindfulness). As well as providing an accessible guide, Anālayo gives a succinct historical survey of the development of mindfulness in Buddhism, and practical exercises on how to develop it.

A wise and helpful presentation of essential elements of the Buddha's teaching . . . it will be of great value for those who wish to put these teachings into practice. A wonderful Dharma gift. – Joseph Goldstein, author of *Mindfulness: A Practical Guide to Awakening*

A gold mine for anyone who is working in the broad field of mindfulness-based programs for addressing health and wellbeing in the face of suffering – in any or all of its guises. – Jon Kabat-Zinn, author of *Meditation Is Not What You Think: Mindfulness and Why It Is So Important*

Bhikkhu Anālayo offers simple skilled mindfulness practices for each of the dimensions of this book. Open-minded practices of embodied mindfulness are described, beginning with eating and health, and continuing with mindfulness examining mind and body, our relation to death, and the nature of the mind itself. Significantly, by highlighting the earliest teachings on internal and external mindfulness, Bhikkhu Anālayo shows how, individually and collectively, we can use mindfulness to bring a liberating understanding to ourselves and to the pressing problems of our global, social, modern world. We need this more than ever. – Jack Kornfield, from the Foreword

ISBN 978 1 911407 57 7
£13.99 / $18.95 / €16.95
176 pages

The Poet's Way

By Manjusvara

From line to rhyme and shape on the page, this accessible guide tackles the essential elements of poetry writing. With imaginative and inspiring exercises, the author illuminates the craft, providing a practical guide to writing and sharpening up your own work.

Featuring Buddhist reflections on the writing process and considering issues such as influence, memory, and the relationship with prayer and ritual, *The Poet's Way* shows how poetry can reveal new aspects of spiritual life.

ISBN 9781 907314 04 9
£8.99 / $12.95 / €12.95

CPSIA information can be obtained
at www.ICGtesting.com
Printed in the USA
JSHW020248210222
23111JS00001B/1